Turkey

Thrace & Marmara p148

İstanbul p58

Black Sea Coast p485

İzmir & the North Aegean p179

Western Anatolia p283

Central Anatolia p400

Northeastern Anatolia p505

Cappadocia p441

Southeastern Anatolia p531

Ephesus, Bodrum & the South Aegean p223

Antalya & the Turquoise Coast p317

Eastern Mediterranean p375

Jessica Lee, Brett Atkinson, Mark Elliott, Steve Fallon,
Virginia Maxwell, Iain Stewart

Contents

PLAN YOUR TRIP

ON THE ROAD

BAKLAVA P44

STATUE, HATAY
ARCHAEOLOGY MUSEUM P395

Contents

RUINS, ANI P524

COVID-19

We have re-checked every business in this book before publication to ensure that it is still open after the COVID-19 outbreak. However, the economic and social impacts of COVID-19 will continue to be felt long after the outbreak has been contained, and many businesses, services and events referenced in this guide may experience ongoing restrictions. Some businesses may be temporarily closed, have changed their opening hours and services, or require bookings; some unfortunately could have closed permanently. We suggest you check with venues before visiting for the latest information.

ON THE ROAD

İSTANBUL TULIP FESTIVAL P119

KAPUTAŞ P342

BLUE MOSQUE, İSTANBUL P70

Contents

UNDERSTAND

SURVIVAL GUIDE

SPECIAL FEATURES

Right: Göreme
(p444)

WELCOME TO
Turkey

You could travel around Turkey hundreds of times and never be bored. In a country overflowing with history and culture, and home to a multi-faceted heritage, there's always something new to discover when I jump on a train or bus and head into the Anatolian heartland. First-time visitors will likely be waylaid by grand old İstanbul's glories and the lush Aegean and Mediterranean coastlines, but my advice is to factor in extra time and strike out from Turkey's western edge to explore.

By Jessica Lee, Writer
🐦 @jessofarabia
For more about our writers, see p639

Turkey

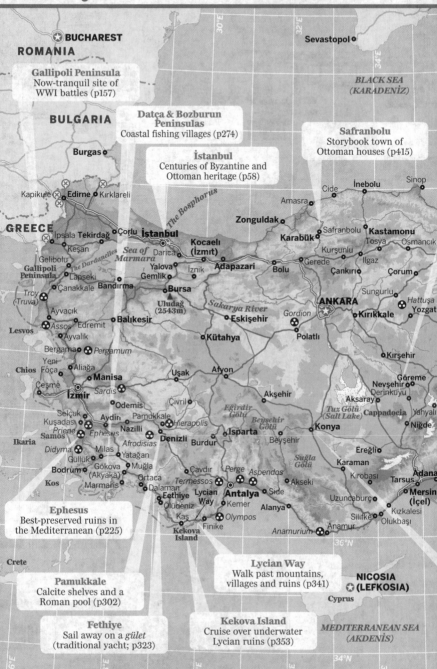

Gallipoli Peninsula
Now-tranquil site of
WWI battles (p157)

**Datça & Bozburun
Peninsulas**
Coastal fishing villages (p274)

İstanbul
Centuries of Byzantine and
Ottoman heritage (p58)

Safranbolu
Storybook town of
Ottoman houses (p415)

Ephesus
Best-preserved ruins in
the Mediterranean (p225)

Lycian Way
Walk past mountains,
villages and ruins (p341)

Pamukkale
Calcite shelves and a
Roman pool (p302)

Fethiye
Sail away on a *gület*
(traditional yacht; p323)

Kekova Island
Cruise over underwater
Lycian ruins (p353)

ROMANIA
BUCHAREST

BLACK SEA
(KARADENİZ)

BULGARIA

Burgas

Sevastopol

Sinop
İnebolu
Cide
Amasra
Zonguldak
Karabük
Safranbolu
Kastamonu
Tosya
Osmancık
Kurşunlu
Ilgaz
Çankırı
Çorum
Sungurlu
Hattuşa
Yozgat
ANKARA
Kırıkkale
Gordion
Eskişehir
Polatlı
Kırşehir
Göreme
Nevşehir
Derinkuyu
Aksaray
Cappadocia
Yahyalı
Niğde

Kapıkule
Edirne
Kırklareli
GREECE
İpsala
Tekirdağ
Keşan
Çorlu
İSTANBUL
The Bosphorus
Kocaeli
(İzmit)
Darıca
Gelibolu
Sea of
Marmara
Yalova
İznik
Adapazarı
Bolu
Gerede
Gallipoli
Peninsula
Lapseki
The Dardanelles
Gemlik
Çanakkale
Bandırma
Bursa
Troy
(Truva)
Uludağ
(2543m)
Sakarya River
Ayvacık
Balıkesir
Kütahya
Lesvos
Assos
Edremit
Ayvalık
Bergama
Pergamum
Yeni
Foça
Aliağa
Uşak
Afyon
Akşehir
Chios
Çeşme
İzmir
Manisa
Sardis
Odemiş
Çivril
Eğirdir
Gölü
Tuz Gölü
(Salt Lake)
Selçuk
Aydın
Pamukkale
Hierapolis
Isparta
Konya
Karaman
Ereğli
Kuşadası
Priene
Ephesus
Nazilli
Denizli
Burdur
Beyşehir
Samos
Afrodisias
Suğla
Gölü
Ikaria
Didyma
Milas
Yatağan
Çavdır
Perge
Aspendos
Akseki
Kırobaşı
Güllük
Gökova
Muğla
Ortaca
Termessos
Adana
Bodrum
(Akyaka)
Dalaman
Fethiye
Lycian
Way
Antalya
Side
Tarsus
Mersin
(İçel)
Kos
Marmaris
Ölüdeniz
Kemer
Alanya
Uzuncaburç
Kızkalesi
Kaş
Olympos
Anamur
Silifke
Olukbaşı
Finike
Anamurium
Ephesus
Kekova
Island
Crete
Beyşehir
Gölü
Kütahya

NICOSIA
(LEFKOSIA)
Cyprus

MEDITERRANEAN SEA
(AKDENİZ)

N 0 — 200 km
0 — 100 miles

36°E
44°N
38°E
40°E
42°N

RUSSIA

Grozny

Ani
Eerie ruins of a former
Armenian capital (p524)

○Sukhumi

GEORGIA

Kutaisi

TBILISI○

⊗Türkgözü

Cappadocia
Surreal fairy chimneys
and cave dwellings (p441)

Kaçkar Mountains
Hike through high-
altitude pastures (p511)

Batumi
Sarp⊗
Hopa○
⊗Aktaş

Vanadzor

○Bafra
Samsun

Ünye
Trabzon Rize○

Mt Kaçkar ○Artvin
(**Kaçkar Dağı**)
(3937m)▲ ○Yusufeli

*Çıldır
Gölü*
Göle○ **Gyumri**○

ARMENIA

YEREVAN○

Sarıkamış
Kars○
*Lake
Sevan*

Giresun
Ordu

○Amasya
Niksar○
Turhal ○**Tokat**
Koyulhisar○

Gümüşhane
Bayburt
○*Sumela
Monastery*

Çoruh River

Kelkit River
Reşadiye
Suşehri
Refahiye

Tortum○ *Aras River* Kağızman○

○Horasan

Tuzluca○ Iğdır○

Mt Ararat
(**Ağrı Dağı**)
(5137m)▲

Zara
Erzincan○ Tercan○

Pasinler○
Erzurum

Ağrı○
Doğubayazıt○ ⊗Gürbulak
Bazargan○

○**Sivas**

Divriği○

Tunceli○
Bingöl○

Patnos○

Muradiye○

IRAN

Kızılırmak River

○Şarkışla

*Keban
Dam*

Elazığ○

Murat River

Mt Nemrut
(**Nemrut Dağı**)
(3050m)▲

Muş
Tatvan○ *Lake Van
(Van Gölü)*

Özalp○

Van○ **Van**○

Kayseri

Gürün○

Karakaya Dam

Bitlis○
Baykan○

Gevaş○
Başkale○

Çatak○

Sero○

Göksun○ Elbistan○
Malatya

Nemrut Dağı
(**Mt Nemrut**)
(2106m)▲

Siirt○

Hakkari○
Mt Cilo
(**Cilo Dağı**)
(4168m)▲

Yüksekova○

Doğanşehir○

Kahta *Atatürk
Dam*

Batman
Diyarbakır Kurtalan○

Şırnak○

○Adıyaman Siverek○
Kahramanmaraş

Hilvan○

Tigris River

○Kozan
Osmaniye ○Karatepe
Gaziantep
(**Antep**)

Birecik○
Viranşehir○
Mardin○

IRAQ

Qamishle○ ⊗
Nussaybin

Ceyhan○
Kilis○

○Barak
○**Şanlıurfa**
(**Urfa**)
⊗Harran ⊗Ceylanpınar

İskenderun○ Öncüpınar⊗ ⊗Elbeyli
Akçakale○

Mosul○

Antakya
(**Hatay**)

○**Aleppo**
(**Halab**)

*Lake
al-Assad*

Nemrut Dağı (Mt Nemrut)
Giant stone heads litter
a mountain (p545)

Erbil○

Reyhanlı
⊗Bab al-Hawa

SYRIA

Kirkük○

Yayladağı⊗
○**Lattakia**

Şanlıurfa
Brilliant museums and the
world's oldest temple (p538)

ELEVATION

Konya
Dervishes whirl at the
Mevlâna Festival (p438)

Antakya
Recharge in Turkey's
'City of Peace' (p395)

*Euphrates
River*

3000m
2500m
2000m
1500m
1000m
700m
500m
200m
100m
0

○**Tripoli**

LEBANON

Palmyra○

BEIRUT○

Turkey's Top Experiences

1 İSTANBUL'S GLORIES

İstanbul is the grand dame of the world's great cities, groaning under the weight of its staggering wealth of Byzantine and Ottoman relics. Architectural highlights range from vast, columned underground Byzantine cisterns to opulent Ottoman palaces liberally decorated with İznik tiles, gild-work and painted panels. Spend a week here and you'll only scratch the surface of the city's glories.

Aya Sofya

For centuries the Aya Sofya (Hagia Sophia) was the greatest church in Christendom. Even in İstanbul, this 6th-century architectural marvel (right), built by Emperor Justinian, stands out. p64

Crossing Continents

Board a commuter ferry and flit between Europe and Asia. Every day, a flotilla of ferries takes locals up the Bosphorus, sharing the strait with tiny fishing boats and massive container ships, all accompanied by flocks of shrieking seagulls. At sunset, the tapering minarets and Byzantine domes of the Old City are thrown into relief against a dusky pink sky – it's the city's most magical sight. p114

Topkapı Palace

This labyrinthine palace (above) was the imperial court of the Ottoman Empire for four centuries. Take in the lavishly painted and tile-clad interiors from where the sultans ruled. p72

2 HISTORIC LANDSCAPES

Every empire-builder worth their salt has swaggered through this land, leaving their mark on the rock-pitted high plateaus, craggy mountain spine and undulating forest-clad hills that roll down to the sea. Amid even Turkey's more remote landscapes, you'll find the signs of human occupation from city ruins perched on mountain slopes to tombs and churches chiselled into the rock, set halfway up high cliffs.

Cappadocia

Fresco-covered Byzantine rock-cut churches hide among the fairy-chimney strewn valleys of Cappadocia (pictured, far right), rock-outcrop castles tower over villages half burrowed into hills, while ever-narrower tunnels lead through multi-leveled underground city complexes below. p441

Gallipoli

Pine-clad hills rise up above Eceabat's harbour and Kilitbahir's castle on this narrow peninsula (left) guarding the entrance to the much-contested Dardanelles. Touring the countryside is a poignant experience: memorials and the passionate guides do a good job of evoking the futility and tragedy of the Gallipoli campaign, one of WWI's worst episodes. p157

Pamukkale

A bleach-white mirage by day and alien ski slope by night, the saucer-shaped calcite shelves of Pamukkale's travertines (above left) have been feted as a natural wonder for centuries with the travertine hill crowned by the spa-city ruins of Hierapolis. p302

3 CLASSICAL RELICS

Tussled over by Ancient Greece and Persia, then trounced by Rome, Turkey is home to some of the world's grandest, biggest and best preserved Classical-era ancient city sites. It's not just all about Greco-Roman ruins, though. Anatolia's homegrown Lycian, Pisidian, Pamphylian, Lydian and Carian (among others) statelets of the Classical era often fused Greek and Persian influences, stamping the remnants of their ancient cities with distinctive Anatolian features.

Ephesus

Turkey's most famous ancient site, Ephesus (Efes) is considered the best-preserved ruin in the Mediterranean. The Library of Celsus (below left) and the frescoes and mosaics inside the Terraced Houses are a tribute to Greek artistry and Roman architectural prowess. p225

AYGUL SARYAROVA/SHUTTERSTOCK ©

Sagalassos

The remains of this ancient city sprawl down a steep mountain slope. In a country where competition is fierce for the title of most dramatically located ruins, Sagalassos (above right) rates near the top. p314

Bergama (Pergamum)

Bergama's Hellenistic theatre is a vertigo-inducing marvel while the Asclepion was Rome's pre-eminent medical centre. p196

Right: Temple of Trajan, Bergama

4 MEDITERRANEAN JOURNEYS

KOJIN/SHUTTERSTOCK ©

KENANOLGUN/GETTY IMAGES ©

ISMAIL BASDAS/SHUTTERSTOCK ©

Backdropped by the hazy contours of the Taurus Mountains, the harbour-front towns of Turkey's Mediterranean coastline are surrounded by pine-clad cliffs hiding horseshoe-shaped coves and fronted by an azure sea, speckled with tiny islands. This scenery is best soaked up from the water. Head out on a boat trip (from towns such as Fethiye, Kaş and Antalya) for lazy sightseeing with isolated beach swim-stops and Mediterranean sunsets to boot.

Gület Cruising

Cruising on a *gület* (traditional wooden yacht) along the Mediterranean's Turquoise Coast is a highlight. The usual route is Fethiye to Olympos, stopping at Mediterranean highlights such as Butterfly Valley but aficionados say the Fethiye to Marmaris route is even prettier. p326

Kekova Island

Kayak or boat over the underwater ruins of Lycian Simena which fringe Kekova island (pictured above), spotting amphorae and building foundations disappearing into the Mediterranean depths, then head to the fort-topped village of Kaleköy, with its harbour of half-sunk Lycian sarcophagi. p353

5 ANATOLIAN KINGDOMS

Hatti ruins, Hittite gates and carved stone reliefs, Urartian fortresses, Phrygian tombs, Pontic remnants, medieval Armenian and Georgian churches, and the mosques and *medreses* (seminaries) of the Seljuk *beyliks* (principalities); amid Anatolia as neighbouring powers pushed and pulled, a roll-call of local kingdoms and mini-statelets rose and fell. Explore further than the famous Greco-Roman ruins to attempt to understand the mind-boggling and complicated history of this land.

Nemrut Dağı

The Commagene Kingdom is forever remembered thanks to the building antics of King Antiochus I. The stone heads atop Nemrut Dağı (top left) are a monumental tribute to one king's hubris. p547

Ani

Rubbing up against the Armenian border, the churches of Ani (below left), once capital of the Armenian Kingdom, sit in isolated, eerie glory, on a high plateau. p524

Hattuşa

Remnants of the fortifications at Hattuşa (above right) tumble across the hillside as a monumental reminder that this rural idyll was once capital of the Bronze Age Hittite Kingdom. p421

6 BEACH TIME

ANDREW MAYOVSKYY/SHUTTERSTOCK ©

MARKETA1982/SHUTTERSTOCK ©

NEJDET DUZEN/SHUTTERSTOCK ©

Patara

Throw down your towel on one of the Mediterranean's longest beaches. Patara (left) offers 18km of white sand and undulating dunes backed by the Lycian ruins of Ancient Patara. p339

Gökçeada

Still off most foreign visitors' radars, the long, soft white-sand strip of Aydıncık Beach on Gökçeada (Gökçe Island) is a windsurfing and kitesurfing hub in summer. p175

Kaputaş

This pale sandy cove backed by high cliffs (left), on the road between Kalkan and Kaş, dropped directly out of a tourist brochure. p342

For many visitors, Turkey is all about hitting the beach. Many of the finest Mediterranean *plajlar* (beaches) dot the Lycian Way footpath, while stretches of Aegean sand offer activities such as windsurfing in Alaçatı, Akyaka and Gökçeada. The Black Sea coast also has its charms and the beaches around the historic towns of Amasra and Sinop are perennially popular with Turkish tourists.

7 CULTURAL HIGHLIGHTS

Yes. Yes. Turkey's glut of world-class ruins, architectural wonders and sweeping landscapes will fill up much of your time, but clear space in your trip to experience the living, breathing culture of Turkey. From tucking into the famed Van breakfast on Kahvaltı Sokak to watching Edirne's oil-wrestling festival, Turkey's cultural offerings are as attractive as its sights.

Watching the Dervishes Whirl

Head to Bursa or Konya to watch the trance-like ritual of the *sema* (whirling dervish ceremony; below left) where dervishes spin to achieve union with God. p435

DERIC OLSCHNER/500PX ©

Hamam Time

After this traditional soak-and-scrub, you'll be cleaner than you ever thought possible. İstanbul's imperial hamams (above right) provide opulent bathing but there are plenty of hamams throughout the country. p117

Meyhanes

A raucous night mixing meze with rakı (aniseed brandy) and live music at a *meyhane* (tavern; right) is a time-honoured Turkish activity. Head to İstanbul's Beyoğlu district for an introduction to *meyhane* nightlife. p131

8 SCENIC SLOW TRAVEL

GALYNA ANDRUSHKO/SHUTTERSTOCK ©

SABINO PARENTE/500PX ©

NADORE/GETTY IMAGES ©

If you're as interested in the journey as the destination, Turkey offers slow-travel adventures ranging from epic mountain and coastal trekking to long train journeys heading east to Kars and Van, where there's little to do but sit back and enjoy the scenery. Simply eschewing domestic flights to instead head overland, or exploring local areas by dolmuş (minibus), will give you a richer experience of this country's people and landscapes.

Lycian Way

Acclaimed among the world's top 10 long-distance walks, the Lycian Way winds through mountains, forests, coastal cliffs and Lycian city-ruins such as Pınara and Xanthos, for 500km between Fethiye and Antalya. p341

Doğu Ekspresi

Turkey's ultimate scenic train journey is the 24 hour–long Doğu Ekspresi, chugging through the mountains and high plateaus between Ankara and Kars. p619

Kaçkar Trekking

Rippling between the Black Sea coast and the Çoruh River, the Kaçkars (above) rise to almost 4000m. Crossing the *yaylalar* (mountain pastures) between hamlets is one of Turkey's top treks. p502

9 MUSEUMS OF THE SOUTHEAST

Unlike many countries where the national museum hoards all the best archaeological finds, Turkey has so many treasures that many provincial museums are world-class. In the south and southeast, in particular, museum-fiends are in for a treat with two of the three most important mosaic museums in the world, and Şanlıurfa's massive museum devoted entirely to the extraordinary story of human history in the local region.

Gaziantep

The Gaziantep Zeugma Mosaic Museum (top left) is home to Hellenistic and Roman mosaics unearthed from nearby Belkis-Zeugma, including many floor mosaics and the iconic 'Gypsy Girl'. p534

Şanlıurfa

The Neolithic site of Göbeklitepe is now world-famous but to get your head around this region's importance, head first to Şanlıurfa Archaeology Museum (bottom left). p538

Antakya

Head to Antakya to view the feted Antioch Mosaics inside Hatay Archaeology Museum (above) and the Necmi Asfuroğlu Archaeology Museum, home to the largest single-piece mosaic ever found. p395

10 BAZAAR SHOPPING

İstanbul's Grand Bazaar

The Old City's commercial hub since 1461, the Grand Bazaar (above left)is a sprawling medieval shopping mall where both treasure and tat can be found. p96

Bursa's Kapalı Çarsı

Once the hub of Bursa's silk-trading heyday, the vaulted *bedestens* (warehouses) and imposing courtyard *hans* (caravanserais) of the Kapalı Çarsı, still bustle with shoppers today. p289

Şanlıurfa's Bazaar

Squeeze your way around other shoppers through the chaotic, narrow lanes of Şanlıurfa's bazaar area (below left) where tiny stalls sell everything from leatherwork and copperware to plastic buckets. p539

Turkey's bazaars are as much about soaking up the atmosphere and architecture and drinking the complimentary *çay* while you chat with shopkeepers, as they are about searching for souvenirs. If you do find something you like, accept that you might not bag the world's best deal, but at least you'll have honed your haggling skills.

Need to Know

For more information, see Survival Guide (p597)

Currency
Türk Lirası (Turkish lira; ₺)

Language
Turkish, Kurdish

Visas
Some nationalities don't need a tourist visa. Most that do can purchase a tourist e-visa online from www.evisa.gov.tr before travelling.

Money
ATMs are widely available. Credit and debit cards are accepted by most businesses in cities and tourist areas.

Mobile Phones
If your mobile phone is unlocked, you can purchase a prepaid SIM card (SIM *kart*) package with credit and data. You'll need your passport when purchasing. Turkish SIM cards can be used in a foreign phone for 120 days.

Time
Eastern European Summer Time all year round (GMT/UTC plus three hours)

When to Go

İstanbul
GO Apr–May, Sep

Eastern Anatolia
GO May–Jun, Sep

Cappadocia
GO May, Sep–Oct

Aegean
GO May–Jun, Sep

Mediterranean
GO Apr, Sep–Oct

Desert, dry climate
Warm to hot summers, mild winters
Mild to hot summers, cold winters

High Season
(Jun–Aug)

➡ Prices and temperatures highest.

➡ Expect crowds, book ahead.

➡ İstanbul's high-season months are April, May, September and October.

➡ Christmas–New Year and Easter also busy.

Shoulder Season
(May & Sep)

➡ Fewer crowds, except during Kurban Bayramı holiday when it falls in this period.

➡ Warm spring and autumn temperatures.

➡ İstanbul's shoulder season is June to August.

Low Season
(Oct–Apr)

➡ October is autumn (fall); spring starts in April.

➡ Accommodation in tourist areas close or offer discounts.

➡ İstanbul's low season is November to mid-March.

Useful Websites

Lonely Planet (www.lonely-planet.com/turkey) Destination information, hotel reviews, traveller forum and more

Turkish Cultural Foundation (www.turkishculture.org) Culture and heritage; useful for archaeological sites.

Go Turkey (www.goturkey.com) Official tourism portal.

Hürriyet Daily News (www.hurriyetdailynews.com) English-language daily news site.

All About Turkey (www.allaboutturkey.com) Multilingual introduction from a professional tour guide.

Important Numbers

Turkey's country code	☏90
International access code	☏00
Ambulance	☏112
Fire	☏110
Police	☏155

Prices in This Book

Between the time of research and this book going to print, the Turkish lira's value has plummeted with Turkey experiencing whopping levels of inflation. By the time you read this, expect the lira prices quoted throughout this book to have doubled, particularly regarding restaurant prices and site entrance fees. Prices quoted in euro remain steady.

For current exchange rates, see www.xe.com. For current exchange rates, see www.xe.com.

Daily Costs

These prices have been updated to reflect current costs in Turkey.

**Budget:
Less than ₺350**

➡ Dorm bed: €10–15

➡ İstanbul–Gallipoli Peninsula bus ticket: ₺110–130

➡ *Balık ekmek* (fish sandwich): ₺20

➡ Boat day trip: ₺120–160

**Midrange:
₺650–1000**

➡ Midrange double room: €40–90

➡ Car hire per day: €25–35

➡ İstanbul–Cappadocia flight: from ₺200

➡ Fish and meze meal: ₺120–180

➡ Major archaeological site entrance: ₺60–120

**Top end:
More than ₺1000**

➡ Double room: more than €90

➡ İstanbul–Cappadocia flight: around ₺450

➡ Private guided site tour: ₺250–350

➡ Four-day *gület* cruise: €200–300

Opening Hours

Standard opening hours:

Tourist information 9am–12.30pm and 1.30pm–5pm Monday to Friday

Restaurants 11am–10pm

Bars 4pm–late

Nightclubs 11pm–late

Shops 9am–6pm Monday to Friday

Government departments, offices and banks 8.30am–noon and 1.30pm–5pm Monday to Friday

Arriving in Turkey

İstanbul Airport Havaist bus HVIST-16 to Taksim (₺35, 1½ hours, every 30 to 60 minutes; 24 hours). To Sultanahmet, take bus HVIST-12 to Beyazıt Meydanı (₺35, 1½ hours, every 25 to 60 minutes, 24 hours) and then the tram (two stops) to Sultanahmet. Taxi to Sultanahmet (₺265) and Beyoğlu (₺255).

Sabiha Gökçen International Airport (İstanbul) Havabus bus to Taksim (₺27.50, 1½ hours, half-hourly 4am to 1am), from where a funicular and tram travel to Sultanahmet (30 minutes); Havabus bus to Kadıköy (₺20, one hour, half-hourly 6.30am to 12.30am); taxi to Sultanahmet (₺260) and Beyoğlu (₺270).

Esenler Otogar (Büyük İstanbul Otogarı; İstanbul) M1 metro to Aksaray then tram from Yusefpaşa to Sultanahmet (₺12); to Taksim Meydanı, take M1 metro to Yenikapı then M2 metro to Taksim (₺12); taxi to Sultanahmet (₺65) and Beyoğlu (₺70).

Getting Around

Air Domestic air routes across Turkey. Buy tickets well in advance to get the best fare.

Bus Efficient and decent value. Extensive network covering the entire country. Fewer services from tourist destinations in winter.

Car Great for rural areas. Drive on the right. Petrol is expensive.

Ferry Regular services cross the Sea of Marmara and link parts of the Aegean coast.

Train The high-speed (YHT) train network currently links İstanbul, Eskişehir, Ankara and Konya. Regular trains stretch across Anatolia from Ankara heading east plus services from major towns such as İzmir and Denizli.

For much more on **getting around**, see p613

First Time Turkey

For more information, see Survival Guide (p597)

Checklist

➡ Check your passport will be valid for at least six months after entering Turkey.

➡ Check if you need a visa and purchase it at www.evisa.gov.tr.

➡ Inform your credit-card provider of your travel plans.

➡ Check travel vaccinations are up to date.

➡ Book flights and hire car online.

➡ Book accommodation for popular areas.

What to Pack

➡ Passport

➡ Paper copy of e-visa as backup

➡ Credit and debit cards

➡ Bank's contact details

➡ Backup euros/dollars

➡ Oral rehydration salts

➡ Conservative clothing (including head scarf for women) for mosque visits

➡ Toilet roll/paper

➡ Soap or hand sanitiser

➡ Chargers and adaptor

➡ Mobile phone

➡ Insurer's contact details

Top Tips for Your Trip

➡ Make an effort to get off the beaten track; village hospitality and home cooking are memorable experiences.

➡ Get to popular sites when they first open in the morning as tour buses generally start arriving around 10am.

➡ In July and August, domestic tourism is in full swing for the summer holidays. Prices are lower and sites less visited if you travel outside this period.

➡ Buying an İstanbulkart in İstanbul provides good discounts on public transport and is required to use the bus system (including the airport bus).

➡ Travellers to Turkey are expected to carry their passport (or national ID card if they used that to enter the country) at all times.

➡ Marches and demonstrations are a regular occurrence, but best avoided as they can lead to clashes with the police.

What to Wear

İstanbul and the Aegean and Mediterranean resort towns are used to Western dress, including bikinis on the beach and short skirts in nightclubs. In eastern and central Anatolia, people are conservative; even men should stick to long trousers. In staunchly Islamic cities such as Erzurum, even T-shirts and sandals are inadvisable. Women do not need to cover their head unless they enter a mosque. To decrease the likelihood of receiving unwanted attention from local men with misconceptions about the 'availability' of Western women, dress on the conservative side throughout Turkey.

Sleeping

It's generally unnecessary to book accommodation in advance. Indeed, walk-in prices are often considerably below advertised rates. Exceptions, however, are high-season peak periods in İstanbul, Bodrum and other resort areas where reserving well ahead can prove wise.

Islam & Ramazan

Turkey is predominantly Islamic, but tolerant of other religions and lifestyles. This is especially true in western Turkey where towns and cities have both mosques and bars, and it is sometimes easy to forget you are in an Islamic country. Do bear in mind, however, that Ramazan (also called Ramadan), the holy month when Muslims fast between dawn and dusk, currently falls around April and May. Cut the locals some slack; they might be grumpy if they are fasting in hot weather. Don't eat, drink or smoke in public during the day, and if you aren't a fasting Muslim, don't go to an *iftar* (evening meal to break the fast) tent for cheap food.

Bargaining

Haggling is common in bazaars as well as for out-of-season accommodation and long taxi journeys. In other instances, you're expected to pay the stated price.

Tipping

Turkey is fairly European in its approach to tipping and you won't be pestered for baksheesh. Tipping is customary in restaurants, hotels and taxis; optional elsewhere.

Restaurants A few coins in budget eateries; 10% of the bill in midrange and top-end establishments.

Hotel porters €2 per bag at midrange hotels; €5 per bag at top-end hotels.

Taxis Round up metered fares to the nearest lira.

LANGUAGE

English and German are both widely spoken in İstanbul and tourist-focused towns along the Mediterranean coast and in Cappadocia; much less so in eastern and central Anatolia where knowing a few Turkish phrases, covering relevant topics such as accommodation and transport, is invaluable. Turkish pronunciation is easy but as it's an agglutinative language where grammatical structure uses strings of suffixes after a trunk word, it can be very difficult to learn. Learning Turkish is more useful than Kurdish, as most Kurds speak Turkish (but not vice versa).

Etiquette

Greetings Turkish friends and family greet each other with either air-kissing or tapping both cheeks. Shaking hands is normal for and between all genders when first meeting people.

Religion Dress modestly and remove shoes when entering mosques. Women should don a headscarf (bring your own or borrow from a box at the entrance).

Politics Be tactful. Politics is a divisive subject in Turkey. Criticising Turkish nationalism can land you in prison.

Alcohol Bars are common in tourist-oriented towns. Public drinking and inebriation are much less acceptable in more conservative areas.

Visiting homes Always remove shoes before entering a Turkish home.

Relationships Do not be overly tactile with your partner in public; beware miscommunications with locals.

What's New

Simultaneously contending with COVID-19, spiralling inflation and natural disasters, Turkey has endured a tumultuous few years. Tourism though, is bouncing back. While foreign visitors focus on İstanbul, the Mediterranean and Cappadocia, local travellers are flocking to cities such as Şanlıurfa, Kars and Antakya: you would do well to follow their lead.

Ancient Buildings, New Mosques

In 2020 the Aya Sofya (Hagia Sophia) and the Kariye Museum (Chora Church) were reconverted from museums into working mosques. Approximately 350,000 worshippers crowded around the Aya Sofya to attend its first Friday prayers in July 2020. For visitors, the new status means some changes (though Kariye Mosque, p104, is closed for restoration, so changes remain to be seen). At the Aya Sofya (p64), entrance is free, visitors should dress respectfully (shoulders and knees covered; women should don a headscarf) and non-Muslims shouldn't enter during prayer times.

Arslantepe

Arslantepe (p549) was anointed as Turkey's newest Unesco World Heritage Site in July 2021. Since then, visitor numbers to this settlement mound, which dates back to the Chalcolithic period, have already increased 10-fold from around 30 per day to 300. Plans are now afoot for building an onsite visitor centre and new protective roof.

Public Transport Updates

Turkey's public transport network (which was great to begin with) keeps getting better.

➡ If you're travelling around the popular summer destinations of Bodrum, Fethiye or Marmaris (or anywhere else in Muğla Province) download the Muğla Kart app onto your phone. This handy new app is a boon for independent travellers, listing all local bus and dolmuş (minibus) routes and timetables for the province.

LOCAL KNOWLEDGE

WHAT'S HAPPENING IN TURKEY

By Jessica Lee, Lonely Planet writer

It's not surprising that politics is at the forefront of most Turks' minds these days. While the government continues touting grandiose, headline-grabbing infrastructure plans, such as the controversial Kanal İstanbul, Turkey's economy as a whole is nose-diving with rampant inflation hitting pockets hard.

Turkey's economic problems have been further exacerbated by COVID-19, which struck Turkey heavily. Although its efficiently handled vaccination rollout is due kudos, by the end of 2021 Turkey was placed sixth highest for case-numbers worldwide throughout the entire pandemic. At the same time, Turkey was struck by several disasters. The October 2020 İzmir earthquake killed 119 and left 15,000 people homeless while in 2021, the Marmara Sea's marine mucilage problem, the Black Sea coast's floods and the Mediterranean coast's forest fires (the worst in Turkish history) brought the subject of Turkey's lack of preparedness and vulnerability to climate change to the fore.

➡ In İstanbul a new tramline links Cibali in the central city with Alibeyköy otogar (bus station) via Fener, Balat and Eyüp. Great news for travellers bussing into İstanbul and anyone who wants to explore the city's Golden Horn sights. The last section of this tramline, linking Cibali to Eminönü, is planned to be completed by the end of 2022, making it even more useful.

➡ In response to the pandemic, in many cities you need to register your HES code to use the city bus/tram/metro network. For details, see p618.

Laodicea

With Pamukkale's Hierapolis ruins nearby, the ancient site of Laodicea (p308) has often been overlooked by travellers but with the grand restoration of Laodicea's west theatre finished in 2021 and the re-erection of a fresco-covered wall at the western end of Syria Street completed in 2020, this ancient site offers plenty of new reasons to visit.

Antakya Mosaics

Construction of a luxury hotel went awry in Antakya when work on the site excavated a haul of mosaics. The result is the new Necmi Asfuroğlu Archaeology Museum (p397; with the hotel 'floating' above the archaeological park), home to the world's largest single-piece mosaic.

Balat Buzz

The Golden Horn neighbourhood of Balat is İstanbul's new cafe-culture hub, with lanes home to freshly painted candy-coloured houses and independent cafes, restaurants and boutique-style shops.

Van Museum

Van's new museum (p560 has finally flung open its doors so travellers can once again view the world's most important collection of Urartian artefacts.

Eskişehir Modern Art

Eskişehir was already known for its lively, youthful energy and progressive spirit so the opening of the Odunpazarı Modern Museum (p297) has simply added to its reputation. The museum, showcasing contemporary art, is a boldly modern addition to the city's historic quarter.

LISTEN, WATCH & FOLLOW

For inspiration and up-to-date news, visit www.lonelyplanet.com/turkey/articles.

Turkish Culture & Tourism Ministry (https://muze.gov.tr) Official website for Turkey's major archaeological sites and museums.

İstanbul Museums (https://muze.gen.tr) Official website for İstanbul's museums and historic sites.

Culinary Backstreets İstanbul (https://culinarybackstreets.com/category/cities-category/istanbul) Food focused dispatches from İstanbul.

@goturkiye The official Turkey Tourism Instagram account.

@duvarenglish Twitter feed with news from across Turkey in English.

FAST FACTS

Food trend Modern Turkish

Annual tea consumption 3.16kg per person

Youth unemployment 24.6%

Population 81.25 million

Göbeklitepe

Göbeklitepe (p539) became an Unesco World Heritage Site in 2018 and since then the site facilities have received a massive upgrade, including a snazzy visitors centre. The Neolithic site is one of southeastern Anatolia's must-see sights – its popularity further egged-on by a starring role in Turkish Netflix drama *Atiye* (renamed *The Gift* in English).

Troy

Troy finally gets a museum (p174) that matches this archaeological site's fame. Neighbouring the ruins, the spectacular Museum of Troy illuminates 4000 years of history and legend.

Accommodation

Find more accommodation reviews throughout the On the Road chapters (from p57)

Accommodation Types

Apartments Mostly found in İstanbul and in coastal spots such as Kaş, Antalya and the Bodrum Peninsula. Generally good value for money, especially for families and small groups.

Boutique hotels Turkey's most interesting accommodation with options to bed down in old Ottoman mansions, caravanserais, cave complexes (in Cappadocia), and other historic buildings.

Camping Campgrounds are fairly prevalent along the coasts but rarer inland. Some pensions and hostels let you camp on their grounds and use their facilities for a fee.

Hostels In areas popular with younger travellers such as İstanbul and Göreme, there are hostels offering dorm beds for less than €20 per night.

Hotels Wide variety from cheap and basic to luxurious. Rates, even in the most basic, nearly always include breakfast.

Pensions (Pansiyons) Family-run guesthouses. Rates and facilities range hugely, from simple but comfortable budget options (often in lesser-visited destinations) to top-end pensions with prices on a par with those of boutique hotels. Meals are often available.

Resorts Generally found at the popular beach destinations along the Aegean and Mediterranean coasts.

PRICE RANGES

Ranges are based on the cost of an ensuite double room including tax and breakfast. The rates we quote are for high season, which generally means June to August, apart from in İstanbul, where high season is April, May, September, October, Christmas and Easter.

İstanbul, İzmir & Bodrum Peninsula

€ less than €80

€€ €80–180

€€€ more than €180

Rest of Turkey

€ less than €25

€€ €25–60

€€€ more than €60

Best Places to Stay

Best on a Budget

In towns that receive a lot of international visitors, *pansiyons* (pensions) and hostels often are the best budget options. There's a plethora of Turkish one- and two-star hotels. The vast majority offer solid facilities and an en-suite double for between ₺120 and ₺180 including breakfast. Booking direct nearly always gets you a better room rate.

➡ Akın House (p124), İstanbul

➡ Tan Pansiyon (p327), Fethiye

➡ Homeros Pension (p239), Selçuk

➡ Odyssey Guesthouse (p200), Bergama

➡ Deeps Hostel (p407), Ankara

Best for Families

Turkey is very family oriented and family rooms (ranging from a simple large quad-bed room to suites with connecting rooms) are common. Although many families will automatically opt to book a resort for a family holiday, many small, locally-owned options provide excellent, family-friendly facilities.

- ➡ Olive Farm Guesthouse (p277), Eski Datça
- ➡ Owlsland (p347), Bezirgan
- ➡ Akay Pension (p340), Patara
- ➡ Caretta Caretta Pension (p358), Çıralı

Best for Solo Travellers

In tourist centres such as İstanbul, Göreme and Selçuk there are great hostel options. Single rooms aren't particularly common but many hotels and pensions do discount the double room rate for solo travellers.

Outside tourist areas, solo travellers of both sexes should be cautious about staying in the very cheapest budget no-star hotels; theft and even sexual assaults have occurred, albeit very rarely.

- ➡ Homestay Cave Hostel (p448), Göreme
- ➡ Ateş Pension (p350), Kaş
- ➡ Taksıyarhis Pansiyon (p190), Ayvalık
- ➡ Liman Hotel (p245), Kuşadası

Best for Boutique Style

These distinctive properties offer a local experience with a stylish twist. Options include half-timbered Ottoman mansions in the old town districts of cities and towns such as Safranbolu, Greek stone-cut houses along the Aegean and Mediterranean coasts, and Cappadocia's cave-hotels where troglodyte living is combined with 21st-century comforts.

- ➡ Sota Cappadocia (p467), Ürgüp
- ➡ Assos Alarga (p186), Behramkale
- ➡ Latife Hanım Konağı (p181), Bozcaada
- ➡ Hotel Empress Zoe (p122), İstanbul

Hotel Empress Zoe (p122)

Booking

During high season in popular destinations such as İstanbul, Bodrum and other coastal resorts, and Göreme it's wise to reserve ahead. Outside of peak periods though, walk-in prices are often below advertised rates and it's generally unnecessary to book in advance. Most accommodation options in cities and tourist-oriented regions have both a website and a presence on the big hotel-booking sites. In lesser-visited regions, some properties still have no internet presence.

Since 2017, the booking.com website has been banned for use within Turkey. Bookings can still be made through the site from outside Turkey (and when using a VPN on your device while in-country).

At Lonely Planet (lonelyplanet.com/hotels) you can fnd independent reviews, as well as recommendations on the best places to stay.

Price Fluctuations

Rooms are discounted by 20% to 50% during low season but not during Christmas and Easter periods and major Islamic holidays. In tourist areas, hoteliers peg their room prices to the euro to insulate their businesses against fluctuations in the lira. Their rates in lira thus rise and fall according to the currency's value against the euro. In contrast, hoteliers in less touristy areas are more likely to simply set their rates in lira – a difference that compounds the already huge regional variations across Turkey.

Hotel prices in İstanbul, along the Mediterranean coast and in Cappadocia in particular can vary wildly, plummeting when security concerns cause international tourism numbers to drop. At times when the security and domestic political situations are stable, hotel prices sharply rise.

Month by Month

January

The dead of winter. Even İstanbul's streets are empty of crowds, local and foreign, and snow closes eastern Anatolia's mountain passes and delays buses. Accommodation in tourist areas is mostly closed.

✨ New Year's Day

A surrogate Christmas takes place across the Islamic country, with decorations, exchanges of gifts and greeting cards. Celebrations begin on New Year's Eve and continue through this public holiday. Over Christmas and New Year, accommodation fills up and prices rise.

March

As in the preceding months, you might have sights to yourself outside the country's top destinations, and you can get discounts at accommodation options that are open.

☆ İzmir European Jazz Festival

This jazz festival fills the Aegean city with a high-profile line-up of European and local performers. Gigs, workshops, seminars and a garden party make this a lively time for jazz lovers to visit. (p209)

📅 Çanakkale Deniz Zaferi

On 18 March, Turks descend on the Gallipoli (Gelibolu) Peninsula and Çanakkale to celebrate what they call the Çanakkale Naval Victory – and commemorate the WWI campaign's 130,000 fatalities. The area, particularly the Turkish memorials in the southern peninsula, is thronged with visitors.

✖ Mesir Macunu Festivalı

An altogether different way of marking the spring equinox, Manisa's Unesco-protected festival celebrates *Mesir macunu* (Mesir paste), a scrumptious treat made from dozens of spices that once cured Süleyman the Magnificent's mother of illness. The festival usually takes place in late March or April. (p215)

April

Spring. April and May are high season in İstanbul and shoulder season elsewhere. Not a great month to get a tan in northern Turkey, but you can enjoy balmy, breezy weather in the southwest.

☆ İstanbul Film Festival

For a filmic fortnight, cinemas around town host a packed program of Turkish and international films and events. An excellent crash course in Turkish cinema, but book ahead. (p119)

✨ İstanbul Tulip Festival

İstanbul's parks and gardens are resplendent with tulips, which originated in Turkey before being exported to the Netherlands during the Ottoman era. Multicoloured tulips are often planted to resemble the Turks' cherished 'evil eye'. Flowers bloom from late March or early April. (p119)

🗓 Anzac Day, Gallipoli Peninsula

On 25 April, the WWI battles for the Dardanelles are commemorated and the Allied soldiers remembered. Antipodean pilgrims sleep at Anzac Cove before the dawn services; a busy time on the peninsula.

May

Another good month to visit. Shoulder season continues outside İstanbul, with attendant savings, but spring is flirting with summer and the Aegean and Mediterranean beaches are heating up.

🏃 Windsurfing, Alaçatı

In Turkey's windsurfing centre, Alaçatı, the season begins in mid-May. The protected Aegean bay hosts the Windsurf World Cup in August and the season winds down in early November, when many of the eight resident schools close. (p220)

👁 Ruins, Mosques, Palaces & Museums

This is your last chance until September to see the main attractions at famous Aegean and Mediterranean sights such as Ephesus (Efes) without major crowds, which can become almost unbearable at the height of summer.

🏃 Dedegöl Dağcılık Şenliği

Now spring is thawing the Taurus Mountains, the Dedegöl Mountaineering Festival sees Eğirdir's mountaineering club scramble up Mt Dedegöl (2998m). Register to join the free two-day event (19 May), which includes a night staying at the base camp.

☆ Uluslararasi Bursa Festivali

The International Bursa Festival, the city's 2½-week music and dance jamboree, features diverse regional and world music, plus an international headliner or two. Free performances are offered and tickets for top acts are around ₺40. Begins in mid-May.

✨ Cappadox Festival, Cappadocia

Cappadocia's biennial three-day arts festival merges music, nature walks, art exhibitions, yoga and gastronomy into an extravaganza of Turkish contemporary culture, highlighting the area's natural beauty.

🍴 International Giresun Aksu Festival

The historical, hazelnut-producing Black Sea town hails fecundity and the new growing season with boat trips to Giresun Island, concerts, traditional dance performances and other open-air events. A week in late May.

June

Summer. Shoulder season in İstanbul and high season elsewhere until the end of August. Expect sizzling temperatures, inflexible hotel prices and crowds at sights – often avoided by visiting early, late or at lunchtime.

✨ Çamlıhemşin Ayder Festival

Held over the first or second weekend in June, this popular early-summer festival in Ayder highlights Hemşin culture with folk dance and music. It also features northeast Turkey's bloodless form of bull-fighting, *boğa güreşleri,* in which two bulls push at each other until one backs off.

🍴 Cherry Season

June is the best month to gobble Turkey's delicious cherries, which Giresun introduced to the rest of the world. Founded more than 2000 years ago as the Greek colony of Cerasus (Kerasos), the Black Sea town's ancient name means 'cherry' in Greek.

☆ İstanbul Music Festival

Probably Turkey's most important arts festival, featuring performances of opera, dance, orchestral concerts and chamber recitals. Acts are often internationally renowned and the action takes place at atmosphere-laden venues such as Aya İrini, the Byzantine church in the Topkapı Palace grounds. (p119)

🤼 Historic Kırkpınar Oil-Wrestling Festival, Edirne

In a sport dating back over 650 years, brawny *pehlivan* (wrestlers) from across Turkey rub themselves from head to foot with olive oil and grapple. Late June or early July. (p151)

🤼 Kafkasör Kültür, Sanat ve Turizm Festivali, Artvin

Join the crush at the *boğa güreşleri* (bloodless bull-wrestling matches) at Artvin's Caucasus Culture, Arts & Tourism Festival, held in the Kafkasör Yaylası pasture, 7km southwest of the northeastern Anatolian mountain town. Late June or early July. (p517)

July

This month and August turn the Aegean and Mediterranean tourist heartlands into sun-and-fun machines, and temperatures peak across the country. The blue skies bring out the best in the Turkish personality.

☆ İstanbul Jazz Festival

Held annually from late June to mid-July, this is an exhilarating hybrid of conventional jazz, electronica, drum and bass, world music and rock. Venues include Nardis Jazz Club in Galata, Salon in Şişhane, and parks around the city.

🏃 Mountain Walking

Between the Black Sea coast and the Anatolian steppe, the snow clears from the passes in the Kaçkar Mountains (Kaçkar Dağları), allowing multiday treks (www.cultureroutesinturkey.com) and sublime *yaylalar* (highland pastures) views throughout July and August.

☆ Music Festivals

Turkey enjoys a string of summer music jamborees, including highbrow festivals in İstanbul, Bursa and İzmir. The cities host multiple pop, rock and dance music events, while summer playgrounds such as Alaçatı and the Bodrum Peninsula turn into mini-Ibizas. June to August.

August

Even at night, the weather is hot and humid; pack sun cream and anti-mosquito spray. Walking and activities are best tackled early in the morning or at sunset.

🤼 Cappadocian Festivals

Two festivals take place in the land of fairy chimneys. A summer series of chamber music concerts are held in the valleys and, from 16 to 18 August, sleepy Hacıbektaş comes alive with the annual pilgrimage of Bektaşi dervishes.

September

İstanbul's second high season begins; elsewhere, it's shoulder season – temperatures, crowds and prices lessen. Accommodation and activities, such as boat trips, begin winding down for the winter.

☆ Aspendos Opera & Ballet Festival

The internationally acclaimed Aspendos Opera & Ballet Festival takes place in this atmospheric Roman theatre near Antalya (June or late August and September). (p370)

🏊 Diving

The water is warmest from May to October and you can expect water temperatures of 25°C in September. Turkey's scuba-diving centre is Kaş on the Mediterranean, with operators also found in Marmaris, Bodrum, Kuşadası and Ayvalık on the Aegean.

☆ Kaş Caz Festival

This delightful Mediterranean coastal town boasts a fine jazz festival in early September, with international and Turkish musicians. Some performances are held in the town's ancient amphitheatre. (p349)

🤼 İstanbul Biennial

The city's major visual-arts shindig, considered to be one of the world's most prestigious biennials, takes place from mid-September to mid-November in odd-numbered years. Venues around town host the internationally curated event. (p119)

October

Autumn is truly here; outside İstanbul, many accommodation options have shut for the winter. Good weather is unlikely up north, but the Mediterranean and Aegean experience fresh, sunny days.

Walking

The weather in eastern Anatolia has already become challenging by this time of year, but in the southwest, autumn and spring are the best seasons to enjoy the scenery without too much sweat on your brow. See www.trekking inturkey.com and www.cariantrail.com.

☆ Akbank Jazz Festival

Every October or November, İstanbul celebrates its love of jazz with this eclectic line-up of local and international performers. Going for over 25 years, it's the older sibling of July's İstanbul Jazz Festival. (p120)

November

Even on the coastlines, summer is a distant memory. Rain falls on İstanbul and the Black Sea, southern resort towns are deserted and eastern Anatolia is ensnarled in snow.

✯ Karagöz Festival, Bursa

A week of performances celebrate the city's Karagöz shadow-puppetry heritage, with local and international puppeteers and marionette performers. Held in November of odd years.

December

Turks fortify themselves against the cold with hot çay and hearty kebaps.

Most of the country is chilly and wet or icy, although the western Mediterranean is milder and day walks there are viable.

🏃 Ski Season

Hit the slopes: the Turkish ski season begins at half a dozen resorts across the country, including Cappadocia's Erciyes Dağı (Mt Erciyes), Uludağ (near Bursa), Palandöken (near Erzurum) and Sarıkamış (near Kars). Late November to early April.

◉ Snow in Anatolia

If you're really lucky, after skiing on Erciyes Dağı, you could head west and see central Cappadocia's fairy chimneys looking even more magical under a layer of snow. Eastern Anatolia is also covered in a white blanket, but temperatures are brutally low.

Itineraries

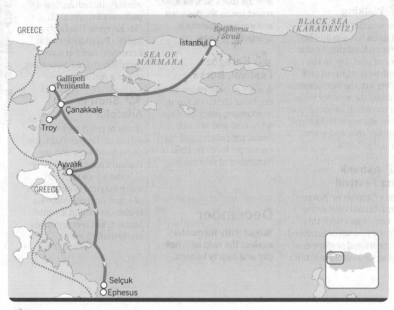

 **Classic Turkey**

Most first-time visitors to Turkey arrive with two ancient names on their lips: İstanbul and Ephesus. This journey across the Sea of Marmara and down the Aegean coast covers both.

You'll need at least three days in **İstanbul** to even scrape the surface of its millennia of history. The top three sights are the Aya Sofya, Topkapı Palace and the Blue Mosque, but there's a sultan's treasury of other sights and activities, including a cruise up the Bosphorus, nightlife around İstiklal Caddesi, and the Grand Bazaar.

From İstanbul, take a bus to **Çanakkale**, a lively student town on the Dardanelles. A tour of the nearby **Gallipoli Peninsula's** poignant WWI battlefields is a memorable experience, as is a visit to the ancient city of **Troy**, immortalised by Homer in his *Iliad*. Don't miss the superb Museum of Troy.

From Çanakkale, it's a 3½-hour bus ride to **Ayvalık**, with its hugely atmospheric old Greek quarter and fish restaurants. Finally, another bus journey (via İzmir) reaches **Selçuk**, a pleasantly rustic town and the base for visiting glorious **Ephesus**, the best-preserved classical city in the eastern Mediterranean.

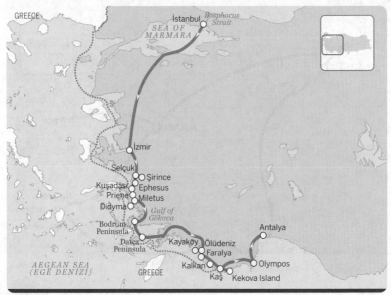

Coastal Cruise

3 WEEKS

Leading across the Sea of Marmara and down the Aegean and Mediterranean coasts, this seaside itinerary takes in beaches, ruins and relaxing holiday towns.

After a few days in İstanbul, fly or bus to **İzmir**, spend a day or two exploring its museums and bazaar, and then catch the bus or train to **Selçuk**. Time your visit to coincide with Selçuk's sprawling Saturday market, and pair the magnificent ruins of **Ephesus** with a trip to the mountaintop village of **Şirince**. Next, hit the southern Aegean coast in cruise port **Kuşadası**, where you can sign up for a 'PMD' day trip to the ruins of **Priene**, **Miletus** and **Didyma**. These sites, respectively two ancient port cities and a temple to Apollo, are interesting additions to an Ephesus visit, giving a fuller picture of the region in centuries past. Spend a day or two nibbling calamari and sipping cocktails on the chi-chi **Bodrum Peninsula** and cross the Gulf of Gökova by ferry to the **Datça Peninsula**. With their fishing villages and rugged hinterland of forested mountains, Datça and the adjoining Bozburun Peninsula are excellent for revving up a scooter or just putting your feet up.

Continuing along the Mediterranean coast, beautiful **Ölüdeniz** is the spot to paraglide from atop Baba Dağ (Mt Baba; 1960m) or lie low on a beach towel. While in the area, consider basing yourself in secluded **Kayaköy** with its ruined Greek town. You're now within kicking distance of the 500km-long Lycian Way. Hike for a day through superb countryside to overnight in heavenly **Faralya**, overlooking Butterfly Valley.

Also on the Lycian Way, the idylllic coastal town of **Kalkan** makes a perfect pit stop, while laid-back **Kaş** has a pretty harbourside square that buzzes nightly with friendly folk enjoying the sea breeze, views, fresh meze and a beer or two. One of Turkey's most beguiling boat trips departs from here, taking in the sunken Lycian city at **Kekova Island**. From Kaş, it's a couple of hours to **Olympos**, famous for the naturally occurring Chimaera flames and rustic beach cabins. A 1½-hour bus journey reaches the city of **Antalya**. Its Roman-Ottoman quarter, Kaleiçi, is worth a wander, against the backdrop of a jaw-dropping mountain range. From Antalya you can fly back to İstanbul or take a nine-hour bus ride across the plains to Cappadocia.

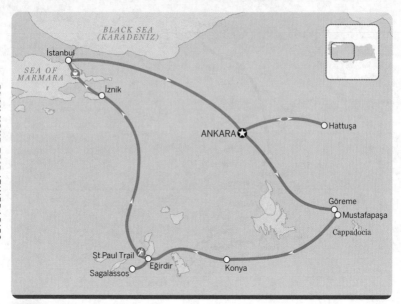

2 WEEKS ## Cappadocia Meander

If you feel drawn to Cappadocia's fairy-tale landscape after İstanbul, and you would like to stop en route across Anatolia, there are a few worthwhile spots to break the journey.

From İstanbul, catch the fast train to **Ankara**, the Turkish capital. The political town is no match for that show-stealer on the Bosphorus, but two key sights here give an insight into Turkish history, ancient and modern: the Anıt Kabir, Atatürk's hilltop mausoleum, and the Museum of Anatolian Civilisations, a restored 15th-century *bedesten* (covered market) packed with finds from the surrounding steppe. Tying in with the latter, a detour east takes in the isolated, evocative ruins of **Hattuşa**, which was the Hittite capital in the late Bronze Age.

Leave three days to explore Cappadocia, based in a cave hotel in **Göreme**, the travellers' hang-out surrounded by valleys of fairy chimneys. The famous rock formations line the roads to sights including Göreme Open-Air Museum's rock-cut frescoed churches and the Byzantine underground cities at Kaymaklı and Derinkuyu. Among the hot-air balloon trips, valley walks and horse riding, schedule some time to just sit and appreciate the fantastical landscape in çay-drinking villages such as **Mustafapaşa**, with its stone-carved Greek houses and 18th-century church.

Fly straight back to İstanbul or, if you have enough time and a penchant for Anatolia's mountains and steppe, continue by bus. Stop in **Konya** for lunch en route to **Eğirdir**, and tour the turquoise-domed Mevlâna Museum, containing the tomb of the Mevlâna (whirling dervish) order's 13th-century founder. Lakeside Eğirdir, with its road-connected island and crumbling old Greek quarter ringed by beaches and the Taurus Mountains (Toros Dağları), is a serene base for walking a section of the **St Paul Trail**. Possible day trips include the stunning ruins of **Sagalassos**, a Graeco-Roman city at 1500m in the Taurus Mountains.

From Eğirdir, you can catch a bus back to İstanbul or fly from nearby Isparta. If spending your last night in Anatolian tranquillity appeals more than the hustle-bustle of İstanbul, head to lakeside **İznik**, its Ottoman tile-making heritage on display between Roman-Byzantine walls. You will have to change buses in Eskişehir or Bursa to get there, while the final leg of the journey is a ferry across the Sea of Marmara to İstanbul.

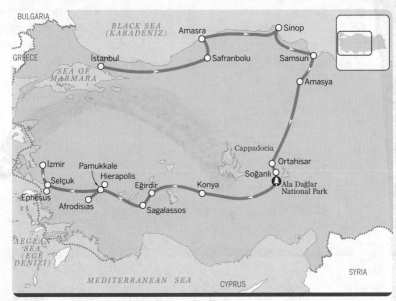

3 WEEKS Anatolian Circle

This trip leaves out only eastern Anatolia, which is a mission in itself, and takes in both obscure gems and prime sights.

Begin with a few days among mosques, palaces and some 20 million folk in **İstanbul**, former capital of the Ottoman and Byzantine Empires. Next, head east to **Safranbolu**, with its winding streets of Ottoman mansions, before turning north to **Amasra**, where Turkish holidaymakers wander the Byzantine castle and eat fresh fish on the two harbours. Amasra is the beginning of the drive through rugged hills to **Sinop**, another pretty Black Sea port town and the birthplace of Greek philosopher Diogenes the Cynic.

Next, it's a six-hour bus journey via **Samsun** to **Amasya**, with its Ottoman houses, Pontic tombs and castle. Take it all in from a terrace by the Yeşilırmak River, and drink several tulip-shaped glasses of çay, before another long bus ride across the Anatolian steppe to Cappadocia. This enchanting land of fairy chimneys and cave churches is wholeheartedly back on the beaten track, but you can escape the tour buses by exploring the valleys on foot or horseback. Likewise, Göreme and Ürgüp are the usual bases, but you could stay in a less-touristy village such as **Ortahisar**, with its craggy castle. South of central Cappadocia, see rock-cut churches without the crowds in **Soğanlı**, where Byzantine monastic settlements occupy two valleys. Then head into the **Ala Dağlar National Park** for some of Turkey's most breathtaking scenery in the Taurus Mountains (Toros Dağları).

Konya, its magnificent mosques recalling its stint as capital of the Seljuk sultanate of Rum, makes a convenient lunch stop en route to Eğirdir. Lakeside **Eğirdir** has views of the Taurus Mountains and little-visited local sights such as **Sagalassos**, a ruined Graeco-Roman city at an altitude of 1500m. There are more impressive classical ruins at **Hierapolis**, an ancient spa city overlooking the village of **Pamukkale** from atop the travertines, a mountain of calcite shelves. Nearby **Afrodisias**, once a Roman provincial capital, is equally incredible; you might have the 30,000-seat stadium to yourself.

From Denizli (near Pamukkale), it's just a few hours' journey by bus or train to **Selçuk**, base for visiting **Ephesus**. From Selçuk, you can fly back to İstanbul from nearby **İzmir**, or continue overland via our Classic Turkey itinerary.

Paragliding at Ölüdeniz (p334)

Plan Your Trip
Activities

Whether you want to sail over archaeological remains, tackle challenging summits or explore the countryside on horseback, Turkey offers superb playgrounds for active travellers from aspiring kayakers to dedicated skiers. Safety standards are good too, provided you stick to reputable operators with qualified, English-speaking staff.

Top Regions

Antalya & the Turquoise Coast

The western Mediterranean offers the widest array of activities, including sea kayaking, boat trips, diving, two waymarked walking trails, canyoning, rafting and paragliding.

Cappadocia

Excellent for a half- or full-day hike, with a surreal landscape of curvy valleys and fairy chimneys. There are also mountain-walking opportunities, horse riding, and skiing on Erciyes Dağı (Mt Erciyes).

Eastern Anatolia

Head to the eastern wilds, especially the northern part, for mountain walking, white-water rafting, horse riding, skiing, snowboarding and cross-country skiing.

South Aegean

Bring your swimming trunks to the more-popular stretch of the Aegean, where operators in spots such as Bodrum, Marmaris and Akyaka offer boat trips galore and water sports including diving, waterskiing, windsurfing and kiteboarding.

Walking & Trekking

Walking in Turkey is increasingly popular among both Turks and travellers, and a growing number of local and foreign firms offer walking holidays here. The country is blessed with numerous mountains, from the Taurus ranges in the southwest to the Kaçkars in the northeast, which all provide fabulous hiking opportunities. Hiking is also the best way to visit villages and sights rarely seen by holidaymakers, and it will give you a taste of life in rural Turkey.

Hiking options range from challenging multiday hikes, such as the 500km St Paul Trail from Perge near Antalya, through rural western Anatolia, and ending near Eğirdir Gölü (Lake Eğirdir), to gentle afternoon strolls, such as in Cappadocia.

For more information on hiking in Turkey, visit Trekking in Turkey (www.trekkinginturkey.com) and Culture Routes in Turkey (www.cultureroutesinturkey.com). Smartphone apps covering Culture Routes' trails can be downloaded from its website.

Safety Advice

Bar a few well-known and well-maintained trails, most are not signposted and it's recommended to hire a guide, or at least seek local advice before setting off.

Weather conditions can fluctuate quickly between extremes, so come prepared and check the local conditions.

Day Walks

For half- and full-day walks, Cappadocia is unbeatable, with a dozen valleys that are easily negotiated on foot, around Göreme as well as the Ihlara Valley. These walks, one to several hours in length with minor gradients, are perfectly suited to casual walkers and even families. The fairy chimneys are unforgettable, and walking is the best way to do the landscapes and sights justice – and discover areas that travellers usually don't reach. After all, there aren't many places in the world where you can walk between a string of ancient, rock-cut churches in a lunar landscape.

Long-Distance Trails

Culture Routes in Turkey has developed two iconic waymarked trails, the Lycian Way and St Paul Trail, plus several new long-distance routes, which range from the Evliya Çelebi Way – tracing the route of the famed Ottoman traveller – to the Carian Trail in the south Aegean. The routes are best tackled in spring or autumn and you don't have to walk them in their entirety; it's easy to bite off a small chunk. Consult the website (www.cultureroutesinturkey.com) for information, guidebooks, apps and maps covering the trails.

Lycian Way

Chosen by British newspaper the *Sunday Times* as one of the world's 10 best walks, the Lycian Way covers 500km between Fethiye and Antalya, partly inland, partly along the coast of ancient Lycia, via Patara, Kalkan, Kaş, Finike, Olympos and Tekirova. Highlights include stunning coastal views, pine and cedar forests, laid-back villages, ruins of ancient cities, Mt Olympos and Baba Dağ (Mt Baba). Kate Clow, who established the trail, describes it in detail in the walking guide *The Lycian Way*.

St Paul Trail

The St Paul Trail extends 500km north, from Perge, 10km east of Antalya, to Yalvaç, northeast of Eğirdir Gölü (Lake Eğirdir). Partly following the route walked by St Paul on his first missionary journey in Asia Minor, it's more challenging than the Lycian Way, with more ascents. Along the way you'll pass canyons, waterfalls, forests, a medieval paved road, Roman baths and an aqueduct, and numerous quaint villages.

St Paul Trail, by Kate Clow and Terry Richardson, describes the trail in detail. Eğirdir is a good place to base yourself, with an activities centre geared towards walking the trail.

Mountain Walks

Turkey is home to some seriously good mountain walking.

Mt Ararat (Ağrı Dağı) Turkey's highest mountain, the majestic and challenging 5137m Mt Ararat, near the Armenian border, is one of the region's top climbs and can be tackled in five days (including acclimatisation) from nearby Doğubayazıt. Note, however, that for most seasons since 2015, the mountain has been officially closed due to security issues. Some ascents were made in 2019, but getting up-to-date local advice is essential. When and if the mountain does open again, you'll also need to be very patient with local bureaucracy.

HOT-AIR BALLOONING

For many travellers, one of Turkey's most iconic outdoor experiences is floating above Cappadocia's undulating waves of rock valleys in a hot-air balloon (p452). The experience is a pricey one and requires a seriously early morning wake-up call but the rolling views of the moonscape below are judged worth it by most travellers. Balloon flights operate year-round but are weather dependent.

Kaçkar Mountains (Kaçkar Dağları) In north-eastern Anatolia, the Kaçkars offer lakes, forests and varied flora, at altitudes from about 2000m to 3937m. There are numerous possible routes, ranging from a few hours to multiday treks crossing the high passes over the mountain range.

Cappadocia The starkly beautiful Ala Dağlar National Park (part of the Taurus Mountains) in southern Cappadocia offers superb multiday trekking opportunities, while 3268m Hasan Dağı (Mt Hasan) can be summited in one challenging day.

Horse Riding

There are numerous opportunities to get on the saddle in Turkey but Cappadocia is Turkey's top spot for horse-riding enthusiasts with numerous good riding tracks criss-crossing the marvellous landscapes. Local outfits offer guided rides from one-hour jaunts to multiday trips. Elsewhere, there are some excellent horse-riding opportunities in the countryside around Fethiye and Antalya (along part of the St Paul Trail), and multiday riding journeys along the trail of the Evliya Çelebi Way.

Water Sports

Lounging on a white-sand beach is certainly tempting, but there are many opportunities to dip your toes in the sea.

Boat Trips

For a boat trip along the Aegean or Mediterranean coast, there are endless possibilities, ranging from day trips – out of pretty much everywhere with a harbour, from Ayvalık in the north Aegean all the way around the coast to Alanya in the eastern Mediterranean – to chartering a graceful *gület* (traditional wooden yacht) for a few days of cruising around beaches and bays. The most popular *gület* route is between Demre (Kale; near Olympos) and Fethiye, although aficionados say the route between Marmaris and Fethiye is prettier.

Sea Kayaking & Canoeing

Maps clearly show the tortuous coastline in the western Mediterranean area, with its secluded coves, deep blue bays, pine-clad mountains, islands shimmering in the distance and laid-back villages. Paddling is the best way to comfortably access pristine terrain – some inaccessible by road – and experience the breathtaking scenery of the aptly named Turquoise Coast. Adding excitement to the journey, you might see flying fish and turtles, and if you're really lucky, frolicking dolphins.

Day trips are the norm, but longer tours can be organised with overnight camping under the stars on deserted beaches. They should include transfers, guides, gear and meals. There are also paddling spots on the Aegean coast, including Akyaka.

Top Paddling Spots

Kekova Sunken City (p353) This magical spot, with Lycian ruins partly submerged 6m below the sea, perfectly lends itself to a sea-kayaking tour from Kaş. This superb day excursion, suitable for all fitness levels, allows you to glide over underwater walls, foundations and staircases submerged by 2nd-century earthquakes, clearly visible through crystal-clear waters.

Patara (p339) Canoeing trips on the Xanthos River offer a unique opportunity to glide past jungle-like riverbanks and discover a rich ecosystem, with birds, crabs and turtles. Ending your journey on Patara beach, Turkey's longest, adds to the appeal.

Paragliding

Picture yourself gracefully drifting over the velvety indigo of the sea, feeling the caress of the breeze... Paragliding from the slopes of Baba Dağ (1960m) in Ölüdeniz, which has consistently excellent uplifting thermals from late April to early November, is top-notch. For beginners, local operators offer tandem flights, for which no training or experience is required. You just have to run a few steps and the rest is entirely controlled by the pilot, to whom you're attached with a harness. Parasailing is also available in Ölüdeniz, while Kaş and Pamukkale are also popular for paragliding.

Diving

OK, the Red Sea it ain't, but where else in the world can you swim over amphorae and broken pottery from ancient shipwrecks? Turkey also offers a wide choice of reefs, drop-offs and caves. The waters are generally calm, with no tides or currents, and visibility averages 20m (not

Horse riding, Cappadocia (p441)

too bad by Mediterranean standards). Pelagics are rare, but small reef species are prolific. Here you can mingle with groupers, dentex, moray eels, sea bream, octopus and parrot fish, as well as the occasional amberjack, barracuda and ray. Around the Gulf of Gökova (p281) between the Bodrum and Datça Peninsulas, it's possible to snorkel with sandbar sharks.

You don't need to be a strong diver; there are sites for all levels of proficiency. For experienced divers, there are superb expanses of red coral to explore (usually under 30m of water).

The standard of diving facilities is high, and you'll find professional dive centres staffed with qualified, English-speaking instructors. Most centres are affiliated with internationally recognised dive organisations. Compared to other countries, diving in Turkey is pretty cheap, and it's also a great place to learn. Most dive companies offer introductory dives for beginners and reasonably priced open-water certification courses.

While it is possible to dive all year, the best time is May to October when the

---

ALTERNATIVE ACTIVITIES

It's not all about the outdoors. For a more relaxing take on activities in Turkey head to the hamam. Hamams are also known as Turkish baths, a name coined by Europeans introduced to their steamy pleasures by the Ottomans. Have a massage or just soak in the calming atmosphere. Some of the best:

Sefa Hamamı (p363) This restored 13th-century gem in Kaleiçi (Old Antalya) retains many of its Seljuk features.

Kılıç Ali Paşa Hamamı (p117) The service matches the stunning interior of this restored 16th-century İstanbul hamam.

Yeni Kaplıca (p292) 'New thermal bath' is actually Bursa's oldest, founded by the 6th-century Byzantine emperor Justinian I.

Cinci Hamam (p417) Famed across Turkey, and a highlight of the heritage town of Safranbolu.

---

water is warmest (you can expect up to 25°C in September).

Kaş is Turkey's scuba-diving hub, with excellent Mediterranean dive sites and numerous operators. On the Aegean coast, Marmaris, Bodrum, Kuşadası and Ayvalık also have a reputation for good diving.

White-Water Rafting

Stick to the more reputable operators, as it's important to choose one with the experience, skills and equipment to run a safe and exciting expedition. Your guide should give you a comprehensive safety talk and paddle training before you launch off downstream.

Winter Sports

Turkey is not just a summer destination. It's still little known outside Turkey that winter sports are widely available here, notably excellent skiing (*kayak* in Turkish).

Skiing

Don't expect the Alps, but powder junkies will be genuinely surprised at the quality of Turkey's infrastructure and the great snow conditions from December to April. Whether you're a seasoned or novice *kayakcı* (skier), there are options galore. Most ski resorts have been upgraded in

recent years and feature good facilities, including well-equipped hotels – and at lower prices than many Western European resorts.

Most hotels offer daily and weekly packages including lift passes and full board. Equipment rental and tuition are available, though English-speaking instructors are hard to find. Most resorts cater to snowboarders, and some offer cross-country skiing and snowshoeing.

Ski Resorts

For information on the following ski resorts and others, check out www.skiing turkey.com.

Uludağ (www.bursa.com.tr; per car ₺15) Near Bursa, this major resort has chain hotels and a gondola from the city's outskirts. On winter weekends it's popular with İstanbullu snow bunnies.

Palandöken (p507) A major resort on the outskirts of Erzurum.

Sarıkamış (Bayraktepe Ski Resort; ☑0474-4136572; www.sarikamisdagas.org; Cıbıltepe Mevki; skipass per day weekdays/weekends ₺30/45) Surrounded by vast expanses of pines, this low-key resort near Kars has deep, dry powder.

Davraz Dağı Mt Davraz rises between three lakes near Eğirdir, offering Nordic and downhill skiing and snowboarding.

Erciyes Dağı (p484) Above Kayseri in the Cappadocia region, Mt Erciyes offers excellent ski runs for all skiing abilities.

Mezes (tapas-like dishes; p44)

Plan Your Trip

Eat & Drink Like a Local

In Turkey, meals are events to be celebrated. The national cuisine is made memorable by the use of fresh seasonal ingredients and a local expertise in grilling meat and fish that has been perfected over centuries. Here, kebaps are succulent, mezes are made daily, and freshly caught fish is expertly cooked over coals and often served unadorned and accompanied by Turkey's famous aniseed-flavoured drink, rakı.

The Year in Food

Spring (March–May)

Kalkan (turbot), *levrek* (sea bass) and *ka-rides* (shrimp) are in plentiful supply. Salads feature broad beans, radish and cucumber; strawberries and green plums are plentiful.

Summer (June–August)

Sardalya (sardines) and *ıstakoz* (lobster) are summer treats. Meze spreads draw on freshly harvested artichoke and walnut. Seasonal salads feature corn and tomato; watermelon and fig start their four-month seasons.

Autumn (September–November)

Locals celebrate the start of the four-month *hamsi* (anchovy), *palamut* (bonito) and *lüfer* (bluefish) seasons, as well as the short *çupra* (gilthead sea bream) season. Pomegranates begin appearing in October.

Winter (December–February)

The best season for fish; December is known for its *hamsi* and January for *istavrit* (horse mackerel). Chestnuts are harvested and roasted on street corners throughout the country.

What to Eat & Drink

Local produce makes its way from ground to table quickly here, ensuring freshness and flavour.

Mezes

Mezes (small, tapas-like dishes) aren't just a type of dish, they're a whole eating experience. If you eat in a local household, your host may put out a few lovingly prepared mezes for guests to nibble on before the main course is served. In *meyhanes* (taverns), waiters heave around enormous trays full of cold mezes that customers can choose from – hot mezes are ordered from the menu. Mezes are usually vegetable based, though seafood dishes can also feature.

Meat

Overall, the Turks are huge meat eaters, which can be a problem if you're a vegetarian. Beef, lamb, mutton, liver and chicken are prepared in a number of ways. The most famous of these is the kebap – *şiş* and döner – but *köfte, saç kavurma* (stir-fried cubed meat dishes) and *güveç* (meat and vegetable stews cooked in a terracotta pot) are just as common.

The most popular sausage in Turkey is the spicy beef *sucuk*. Garlicky *pastırma* (pressed beef preserved in spices) is regularly used as an accompaniment to egg dishes; it's occasionally served with warm hummus (chickpea, tahini and lemon dip) as a meze.

Fish

Fish is wonderful here, but can be pricey. In a *balık restoran* (fish restaurant) you should always try to do as the locals do and choose your own fish from the display. After doing this, the fish will be weighed, and the price computed at the day's per kilogram rate.

Popular species include *hamsi* (anchovy), *lüfer* (bluefish), *kalkan* (turbot), *levrek* (sea bass), *lahos* (white grouper), *mezgit* (whiting), *çupra* (gilthead sea bream) and *palamut* (bonito).

Vegetables & Salads

Turks love vegetables, eating them fresh in summer and pickling them for winter (*turşu* means pickled vegetables). There are two particularly Turkish ways of preparing vegetables: the first is known as *zeytinyağlı* (sautéed in olive oil) and the second *dolma* (stuffed with rice or meat). Simplicity is the key to Turkish *salata* (salads), with crunchy fresh ingredients being adorned with a shake of oil and vinegar at the table and eaten with gusto as a meze or as an accompaniment to a meat or fish main course.

Sugar, Spice & Everything Nice

Turks don't usually finish their meal with a dessert, preferring to serve fruit as a finale. Most of them love a mid-afternoon sugar hit, though, and will often pop into a *muhallebici* (milk-pudding shop), *pastane* (cake shop) or *baklavacı* (baklava shop) for a piece of syrup-drenched baklava, a plate of chocolate-crowned profiteroles or a *fırın sütlaç* (rice pudding) tasting of milk, sugar and just a hint of exotic spices. Other sweet specialities worth sampling are *kadayıf,* dough soaked in syrup and topped with a layer of *kaymak* (clotted cream); *künefe,* layers of *kadayıf* cemented together with sweet cheese, doused in syrup and served hot with a sprinkling of pistachio; and *katmer,* thin layers of pastry filled with *kaymak* and pistachio and served hot.

Drinks

Drinking çay is the national pastime, and the country's cup of choice is made with leaves from the Black Sea region. Sugar cubes are the only accompaniment. The wholly chemical *elma çay* (apple tea) is caffeine-free and only for tourists – locals wouldn't be seen dead drinking the stuff.

Türk kahvesi (Turkish coffee) is a thick brew drunk in a couple of short sips. If you order a cup, you will be asked how sweet you like it – *çok şekerli* means 'very sweet', *orta şekerli* 'middling', *az şekerli* 'slightly sweet' and *şekersiz* or *sade* 'not at all'.

Ayran is a drink made by whipping yoghurt with water and salt; it's the traditional accompaniment to kebaps. *Sahlep* is a hot milky drink made from wild orchid bulbs.

Turkey's most beloved tipple is rakı, a grape spirit infused with aniseed. It's served in thin glasses and drunk neat or with water, which turns the clear liquid chalky white; if you want to add ice *(buz),* do so after adding water, as dropping ice straight into rakı kills its flavour.

Turkish coffee and baklava

Ahmet Bey Yöresel Ev Yemekleri (p551) Head to Malatya for a flavourful romp through a fine range of authentic southeastern cuisine.

Limon (p266) On the Bodrum Peninsula, Limon offers an original take on the much-loved Aegean meze-and-seafood experience.

Van Kahvaltı (p562) Head to the eastern city of Van for the world's best breakfasts. We're not kidding.

Food Experiences

Turkey has epicurean indulgence nailed, from street snacks to gourmet restaurants and every region offers local dishes.

Meals of a Lifetime

Cappadocia Home Cooking (p474) Cooking classes and rustic meals enjoyed in a family home on the edge of the Ayvalı Gorge.

Lâl Girit Mutfağı (p195) Magnificent Cretan-style mezes made in Cunda using recipes from a beloved grandmother.

Orfoz (p263) This Bodrum institution serves unusual and delectable seafood dishes on a terrace with fine coastal views.

Cheap Treats

Balık ekmek Grilled fish fillets stuffed into bread with salad and a squeeze of lemon; sold at stands next to ferry docks around the country.

Simit Bread ring studded with sesame seeds; sold in bakeries and by street vendors.

Midye dolma Mussels stuffed with spiced rice and sold by street vendors.

Döner kebap Lamb cooked on a revolving upright skewer then thinly sliced and served in bread with salad and a sprinkling of sumac.

Gözleme Thin savoury pancakes filled with cheese, spinach, mushroom or potato; particularly popular in central Anatolia.

ESIN DENIZ/SHUTTERSTOCK ©

Above: *Börek* (pastry) with spinach and cheese

Left: *Boza* (fermented-barley drink)

Tost Toasted sandwich filled with cheese and spicy sausage.

Pide The long, thin Turkish take on pizza.

Dare to Try

Kokoreç Seasoned lamb/mutton intestines stuffed with offal, grilled over coals and served in bread; sold at *kokoreçis* (*kokoreç* stands).

Boza Viscous tonic made from water, sugar and fermented barley that has a reputation for building up strength and virility. Try it at historic Vefa Bozacısı (p131) in İstanbul.

Kelle paça Slow-boiled soup of trotters, heads and other unfashionable parts of a sheep. Seen as a hangover cure.

Şalgam suyu Sour, crimson-coloured juice made by boiling turnips or purple carrots and adding vinegar; particularly popular in the eastern Mediterranean city of Mersin.

Tavuk göğsü Sweet milk pudding made with chicken-breast meat.

Söğüş Poached tongue, cheek and brain served cold in bread with chopped onion, parsley, mint, tomato, cumin and hot chilli flakes. A specialty of İzmir.

Local Specialities

İstanbul

It's the national capital in all but name and Turks relocate here from every corner of the country, meaning that regional cuisines are well represented within the local restaurant scene. The Syrian-influenced dishes of Turkey's southeast are particularly fashionable at the moment, but the number one choice when it comes to dining out is almost inevitably a Black Sea–style fish restaurant or *meyhane* (tavern). The only dishes that can be said to be unique to the city are those served at Ottoman restaurants where the rich concoctions enjoyed by the sultans and their courtiers are re-created.

Thrace & Marmara

In Marmara – and especially in its capital, Edirne – liver reigns supreme and is usually served deep-fried with crispy fried chillies and a dollop of yoghurt. Dishes in Thrace are dominated by fish rather

WHEN TO EAT

Kahvaltı (breakfast) Usually eaten at home or in a hotel, although *börek* (sweet or savoury filled pastries) and *simit* (a sesame-encrusted bread ring) make popular eat-on-the-run alternatives.

Öğle yemeği (lunch) Usually eaten at a cafe, *lokanta* (eatery serving ready-made food) or fast-food stand around noon.

Akşam yemeği (dinner) The main meal of the day, typically eaten with family and/or friends around 6pm (rural areas) and 7.30pm to 8pm (cities).

than offal, and the locals are fond of sweet treats such as Gökçeada island's *efi badem* (sugar-dusted biscuits made with almond, butter and flour). In recent years, local wineries here have been producing some of the country's most impressive vintages and can be visited by following the Thracian Wine Route (p156).

The Aegean

Mezes made with seafood, freshly picked vegetables, wild herbs and locally produced olive oil are the backbone of Turkish Aegean cuisine. Fish dominates menus on the coast, but inland villagers love their lamb, serving it in unusual forms such as *keşkek* (minced with coarse, pounded wheat). The island of Bozcada is dotted with picturesque vineyards supplying its well-regarded local wineries with grapes, and wines from the İzmir region are starting to develop a national profile.

Western & Central Anatolia

Turkey's heartland has a cuisine dominated by kebaps. Regional specialities that have become national treasures include the rich and addictive İskender, or Bursa, kebap (döner lamb on a bed of crumbled pide, topped with yoghurt, hot tomato sauce and browned butter) and the *tokat kebap* (skewers of lamb and sliced eggplant hung vertically, grilled, then baked in a wood-fired oven and served with roasted garlic). Both take their names from the cities where they originated.

MENU DECODER

Ana yemekler Main courses; usually meat or fish dishes.

Bira Beer; the most popular local tipple is Efes Pilsen.

Dolma Something stuffed with rice and/or meat.

İçmekler Drinks.

Meze Small tapas-like hot or cold dish eaten at the start of a meal.

Porsiyon Portion, helping. *Yarım porsiyon* is a half portion.

(Kırmızı/Beyaz) Şarap (Red/White) Wine.

Servis ücreti Service charge.

Su Water; *maden suyu* is mineral water.

Tatlı(lar) Sweets; often baklava, stewed fruit or a milk-based pudding.

Zeytinyağlı Food cooked in olive oil.

The Mediterranean

The eastern Mediterranean is home to three towns with serious foodie credentials. Silifke is known for its yoghurt, Adana for its eponymously titled kebap (minced beef or lamb mixed with powdered red pepper then grilled on a skewer and dusted with slightly sour sumac) and Antakya for its wealth of Syrian-influenced dips, salads, croquettes and desserts. The best-loved of these desserts is *künefe*, layers of vermicelli-like noodles cemented together with sweet cheese, doused in sugar syrup and served hot with a sprinkling of pistachio. Both gooey and crispy, it's dangerously addictive – consider yourself warned.

Black Sea Coast

Hamsi (anchovies) are loved with a passion along the Black Sea coast. The classic preparation is to dust them with flour and flash-fry them whole, but local cooks also use this slim silver fish in soups, pilafs and even breads. The rain-soaked slopes that face the sea produce a rich harvest of hazelnuts around Ordu and tea in Rize. Bulgur wheat often stands in for rice and cornmeal finds its way into local dishes like *mıhlama* (a thick cheese fondue that's known as *kuymak* in Trabzon). Local pastries are renowned, notably the decadently rich *Laz böreği* (flaky pastry layered with custard and hazelnuts).

Northeastern Anatolia

Flowery honey from small producers is slathered on bread and topped with ultra-creamy *kaymak* (clotted cream) in a northeastern breakfast ritual that is now emulated across the country. Certain roasted or stewed lamb dishes are reminiscent of those served in neighbouring Iran, Georgia and Armenia, while the Kars region is famed for its roast goose *(kaz)*. Milk from animals grazed on rich upland steppe grasses is used to make many delicious varieties of cheese, while many of the river valleys yield fresh trout. An unusual local soft drink is *reyhane*, flavoured with basil.

Southeastern Anatolia

Top of this region's foodie hit parade is Gaziantep (Antep), destination of choice for lovers of pistachio. The local examples are showcased in the city's famous baklava and *katmer* (thin pastry sheets layered with clotted cream and nuts, topped with pistachio, baked and served straight from the oven). Also notable is Şanlıurfa (Urfa), home to *urfa kebap* (skewered lamb with tomatoes, sliced onion and hot peppers) and the country's best examples of the Arabic-influenced wafer-thin pizza known as *lahmacun*.

Plan Your Trip
Family Travel

Çocuklar (children) are the beloved centrepiece of family life in
Turkey and your children will be welcomed wherever they go. Your
journey will be peppered with exclamations of Maşallah (glory be
to God) and your children will be clutched into the adoring arms of
strangers.

Children Will Love...
Unique Sleeps

Cave hotels, Cappadocia (p448) Bigger kids and
teenagers will enjoy the modern troglodyte experience of bedding down underground.

Gület cruising, Mediterranean coast (p326)
Sleep under the stars aboard a gület (traditional
wooden yacht) on an overnight trip heading out
from coastal towns such as Fethiye, Kalkan
and Kaş.

Gelemiş pensions, Patara (p340) The family-
friendly pensions, with pools, in teensy Gelemiş
village are a relaxing beach-break alternative to
Turkey's big resorts.

Guesthouses, Çıralı (p358) This beachfront village has plentiful guesthouses and bungalows; it's
another chilled-out choice for fun-and-sun family
holidays away from the big-brand resorts.

Exploring Turkish Food

Cappadocia Home Cooking, Ayvalı (p474)
Budding cooks will love learning to cook mantı
(Turkish ravioli) and other Anatolian dishes in this
family home.

Only in İzmir Culinary Walk, İzmir (p208) En-
courage adventurous eating with this full-on jaunt
through İzmir's food scene. The walk is decently
flat so good for those with tots in strollers too.

Culinary Kaş, Kaş (p349) Learn to cook a
Turkish feast together as a family at these daily
workshops.

Best Regions for Kids
İstanbul
Ice cream by the Bosphorus, ferry rides, exploring
the Grand Bazaar.

South Aegean
Ruins such as Ephesus for older children, plus
beaches for kids of all ages. Holiday spots like
Kuşadası, Bodrum, Marmaris and Akyaka offer
facilities, resorts, water parks and sports, with
sights and less touristy coastline nearby.

Turquoise Coast
Water sports and activities from tandem paragliding to sea kayaking over submerged ruins. With
younger children, holiday towns like Kaş offer
picturesque lanes and sandy beaches.

Cappadocia
The fantastical landscape of fairy chimneys (rock
formations) and underground cities will thrill older
children, as will cave accommodation. Outdoor
activities include hikes, horse rides and hot-air
ballooning.

İzmir & the North Aegean
More Aegean beaches. İzmir's kordon (seafront)
is a child-friendly promenade – plenty of space
in which to expend energy and take horse-and-
carriage rides. Boat trips and snorkelling are also
popular.

PAUL BIRIS/GETTY IMAGES ©

Güllüdere (Rose) Valley (p445), Cappadocia

Culinary Backstreets, İstanbul (p118) The 'Shop, Cook & Feast' tour is a great introduction to Turkish cuisine for kids of all ages.

Discovering History

Ephesus, Selçuk (p225) The ultimate site to introduce kids to history with a theatre and odeon to scramble up, Graeco-Roman communal latrines to gross-out at and amazingly restored monuments to gawp at.

Kaymaklı Underground City, Cappadocia (p463) Delving deep underground into Kaymaklı's caverns and tunnels will fascinate most children.

Pamukkale travertines, Pamukkale (p302) After rambling through the ruins of Roman spa town Hierapolis, kids will love walking down the other-worldly white calcite travertines and wading through the turquoise-blue pools along the way.

Basilica Cistern, İstanbul (p83) Kids will love the creepy atmosphere of this subterranean cavern with walkways suspended over the water.

Ancient Patara, Patara (p340) The Lycian ruins of ancient Patara ramble all the way down to the beach, great for mixing swimming and sand fun with some history.

Grand Bazaar, İstanbul (p96) For you it may be all about shopping but for little ones this is a magical labyrinth of colourful lanterns, secret corners and free *lokum* (Turkish delight) dished out by shopkeepers who dote on children.

Getting Outside

Tandem paragliding, Ölüdeniz (p334) Adventurous older children and teens can break up the relaxed beachy vibes with the adrenaline buzz of jumping off Baba Dağ.

Horse riding, Cappadocia (p447) Outdoorsy kids will enjoy exploring the Cappadocia valleys on horseback.

Cable car, Uludağ (p294) When traipsing around Bursa's fine Ottoman relics begins to bore, take the kids up the world's longest cable car.

Eğirdir Outdoor Centre, Eğirdir (p311) Rent bikes to head out on a family cycling trip or explore the lake by boat.

Ferry rides, İstanbul (p110) Let kids get an outdoor geography lesson, complete with great city views and the chance of spotting dolphins on the 25-minute ferry ride between Europe and Asia.

Dragoman tours, Kaş (p348) Lots of outdoor activities that active teens will enjoy, including stand up paddleboarding (SUP), guided snorkelling, boat tours and kayaking.

Good to Know

Look out for the 👶 icon for family-friendly suggestions throughout this guide.

➡ Public baby-changing facilities are rare, and usually only found in malls and some chain restaurants.

➡ Breastfeeding in public is uncommon; best to do so in a private or discreet place.

➡ Cities, towns and even bigger villages have parks with playground equipment, though sometimes it's in dire condition; always check the equipment for safety.

➡ Long-distance buses don't have on-board toilets. Instead they stop for breaks approximately every three hours.

➡ Free travel for children under six on public transport within cities, and discounts on long-distance bus and train journeys are common.

➡ Most car-rental companies can provide baby seats for a small extra charge.

➡ Skinny pavements in old districts of cities and uneven surfaces can make manoeuvring strollers difficult. Be vigilant when crossing roads; drivers rarely stop at pedestrian crossings.

➡ A 'baby backpack' is useful for walking around sights.

➡ Double-check the suitability of prescriptions your children are given while in Turkey.

➡ Pasteurised UHT milk is sold in cartons everywhere but fresh milk is harder to find.

➡ Consider bringing a supply of baby food – what little you find here, your baby will likely find inedible – or it will just be mashed banana.

➡ Migros supermarkets have the best range of baby food.

➡ Most supermarkets stock formula (although it is very expensive) and vitamin-fortified rice cereal.

➡ Disposable *bebek bezi* (nappies or diapers) are readily available.

➡ The best nappies are Prima and Huggies, sold in pharmacies and supermarkets; don't bother with cheaper local brands.

Useful Resources

Lonely Planet Kids (www.lonelyplanetkids.com) Loads of activities and great family travel blog content.

Kids' Corner

Say What?

Hello.	Merhaba. *mer·ha·ba*
Goodbye.	Hoşçakal. (if you're going) hosh·*cha*·kal Güle güle. (if you're staying) gew·*le* gew·*le*
Thank you.	Teşekkür ederim. te·shek·*kewr* e·*de*·reem
My name is ...	Benim adım ... be·*neem* a·*duhm*...

Did You Know? ℹ

- Turks eat triple their body weight in bread annually.
- St Nicholas (aka Santa Claus) was born in Patara.

Have You Tried?

Lokum
Turkish delight

Regions at a Glance

Given Turkey's vast scale, it makes sense to focus your travels on one or two regions. A visit to mighty İstanbul can easily be paired with a bus or train to western Turkey's many highlights, or a flight east for off-the-beaten-track adventures. While there are many constants throughout Turkey and the food is certainly excellent everywhere, this is an incredibly diverse country offering varied experiences. Each region has its own charms, so choose wisely and you could find yourself hiking across snowy mountains in wild northeastern Anatolia, sauntering through cosmopolitan İstanbul or sunbathing on a Mediterranean beach.

İstanbul

History
Nightlife
Shopping

Imperial Grandeur

The megacity formerly known as Constantinople and Byzantium was the capital of a series of empires. The Aya Sofya, a church-turned-mosque-turned-museum-mosque, is the grandest remnant of the Byzantine Empire; Ottoman landmarks include the Blue Mosque and Topkapı Palace.

Beyoğlu Bars

Between the dusk and dawn calls to prayer, up-for-it crowds swirl through Beyoğlu's hole-in-the-wall cocktail bars, rooftop watering holes, pedestrian precincts and bohemian nightclubs.

Markets & Bazaars

The city's bazaars include the sprawling Grand Bazaar, the fragrant Spice Bazaar, and the Arasta Bazaar with its carpet and ceramics stores. There are markets galore, including Kadıköy's food market on the Asian side, while neighbourhoods worth visiting range from Çukurcuma, with its antiques to Tophane for contemporary design.

p58

Thrace & Marmara

Military History
Architecture
Aegean Culture

WWI Battlefields

Over 100,000 soldiers died on the now-tranquil Gallipoli (Gelibolu) Peninsula, a pilgrimage site for Australians, New Zealanders and Turks. Touring the memorials, battlefields and trenches that dot the beaches and hills is simply heart-wrenching.

Ottoman Finery

Edirne's Ottoman gems include Selimiye Mosque, one of the finest works of the great architect Mimar Sinan, while Çanakkale's Ottoman old town has mosques, hamams and a 19th-century clock tower.

Greek Connections

Turkey's northwest corner is famous for the ruined classical city of Troy, which traded with the Greeks until the Trojan War. The excellent Museum of Troy is a superb introduction to the nearby archaeological ruins. A ferry ride from Gallipoli or Çanakkale reaches Gökçeada, with its slow-paced Aegean lifestyle and Greek heritage including hilltop villages.

p148

İzmir & the North Aegean

History
Slow Travel
Food

Multicultural Footsteps

Many peoples have left their mark here. Ayvalık and Bozcaada town's old Greek quarters resonate with memories of the population exchange with Greece, while İzmir has Sephardic synagogues and Levantine architecture. Going further back, the hilltop ruins of Pergamum are some of Turkey's finest, and numerous, less-visited sites are found on the Biga Peninsula.

Village Life

Outside summer, life has a slow rural pace in laid-back spots such as Bozcaada island, the Biga Peninsula, Behramkale, Ayvalık and Bergama. Changing seasons and weekly markets are still the main events.

Meze & Seafood

This is the place to try a classic Turkish feast of meze, *balık* (fish) and rakı (aniseed brandy) on a seafront terrace. If the fish prices seem steep, stick to the olive oil–soaked mezes.

p179

Ephesus, Bodrum & the South Aegean

History
Nightlife
Sun & Surf

Classical Sites

Romans once bustled along the Curetes Way at Ephesus (Efes), Turkey's most visited ruins. Less-frequented sites include eerie Priene, a hilltop Ionian city; Miletus, an ancient port; Didyma's Temple of Apollo, once the world's second-largest temple; and Knidos, a Dorian port on the Datça Peninsula.

Sundowners in Style

Bodrum's tourist machine has created a mean nightlife, with waterfront bar-clubs on its twin bays. Another sexy Bodrum Peninsula sundowner spot is Göltürkbükü, the summer playground of İstanbul's jet set.

Hidden Beaches

The Datça and Bozburun Peninsulas hide secluded coves, while *gület* (traditional wooden yacht) cruises discover unspoilt parts of the coastline between Marmaris and Fethiye.

p223

Western Anatolia

History
Ruins
Activities

Ancient Empires

Bursa was the Ottoman capital before Constantinople, İznik's weathered stone gates and Aya Sofya recall its Byzantine greatness, and the Phrygian Valley's rock-hewn monuments survive from the distant Phrygian era. Meanwhile, Eskişehir mixes its pastel-painted Ottoman quarter with today's lively cultural scene and nightlife.

Mountaintop Relics

Hierapolis, a ruined spa city, famously stands atop Pamukkale's glistening white travertines. Quieter sites include Sagalassos, a Pisidian-Hellenistic-Roman city in the Taurus Mountains, and Afrodisias, a grand provincial Roman capital.

Hiking

Two long-distance hiking paths, the Phrygian Way and St Paul Trail, respectively wind through the Phrygian Valley, and over the Taurus Mountains from the Mediterranean to western Anatolia's serene Lake District.

p283

Antalya & the Turquoise Coast

Beaches
Hiking
Ruins

Sand & Sights

Patara, Turkey's longest beach, and the Dalyan area both offer a diverse menu of sand, ancient ruins and nesting sea turtles. Likewise, as well as its beach, Olympos is famed for its Lycian ruins and the naturally occurring flames of the Chimaera. In Ölüdeniz, see the stunning beach and lagoon from above on a tandem paragliding flight.

Historic Footsteps

The western Mediterranean region's two long-distance waymarked footpaths, the Lycian Way and St Paul Trail, name-check historical folk who passed through. The former trail crosses the Teke Peninsula, littered with sepulchres and sarcophagi left millennia ago by the Lycians.

Lycian Relics

The trademark funerary monuments of the Lycian civilisation nestle in the secluded coves and wrinkly cliff faces of spectacular spots such as Xanthos, Pınara and Kaleköy.

p317

Eastern Mediterranean

History
Cuisine
Biblical Legacies

Surreal Sights

History has a fairy-tale quality here: Kızkalesi Castle (Maiden's Castle) seemingly floats offshore, Zeus is said to have imprisoned hydra-headed Typhon in the Pit of Hell, and Anemurium's sprawling and eerily quiet Roman-Byzantine ruins stretch 500m down to a pebble beach with mammoth city walls scaling the mountainside above.

Arab Influences

Antakya is a Turkish and Arab culinary melting pot. The city's influences from nearby Syria include lemon wedges and mint, which accompany kebaps and local specialities, and hummus abounds.

Paul's Footsteps

The early Christian and Old Testament sites in Tarsus include St Paul's ruined house, where pilgrims drink from the well. Paul and Peter both preached in Antakya (the biblical Antioch), and Silifke's Cave Church of St Thecla recalls Paul's early follower.

p375

Central Anatolia	Cappadocia	Black Sea Coast
History	History	History
Architecture	Activities	Slow Travel
Ruins	Landscapes	Scenery

Momentous Events

This is where Alexander the Great cut the Gordion knot, King Midas turned everything to gold, Atatürk began his revolution, the whirling dervishes first whirled, and Julius Caesar uttered his famous line: *'Veni, vidi, vici'* ('I came, I saw, I conquered').

Ottoman Heritage

Safranbolu and Amasya are Ottoman heritage towns, with boutique hotels occupying their half-timbered, black-and-white houses.

Iconic Sights

Gordion's Phrygian tomb (c 700 BC) might be the world's oldest wooden structure, Sultanhanı is Anatolia's largest remaining Seljuk *han* (caravanserai), and Hattuşa was the Hittite capital over 3000 years ago. Locals say the doorways of Divriği's 780-year-old mosque complex, with their exploding stone stars, are so intricately carved that their artistry proves the existence of God.

p400

Byzantine Christians

Cappadocia was a refuge for Byzantine Christians, who carved monastic settlements into the rock, left frescoes on the cave walls and hid from Islamic armies in underground cities.

Hiking

This is one of Turkey's best regions for going walkabout, with options ranging from gentle saunters through the dreamy valleys to serious missions. South of leafy Ihlara Valley, Hasan Daği (Mt Hasan; 3268m) and the Ala Dağlar National Park are both challenging.

Rock Formations

Cappadocia's lava-formed tuff cliff faces and surreal 'fairy chimneys' are riddled with caves. Some are occupied by centuries-old churches, others by full-time cave-dwellers. Many are now hotels, offering an experience of the troglodyte lifestyle in comfort and style. A memorable way to appreciate the surreal rocky canyons is from above, on a dawn hot-air balloon flight.

p441

Byzantine & Greek

Anatolia's north coast was once the Kingdom of Pontus, and Ottoman Greeks tried to create a post-WWI Pontic state here. Impressive ruins include Sumela, the Byzantine monastery clinging to a cliff face, and Trabzon's 13th-century church-turned-mosque Aya Sofya.

Local Life

Some of the prettiest Black Sea towns, like Amasra and Ünye, attract local tourists but few foreigners. Others like İnebolu and Giresun have great little old cores to discover yet are bypassed by almost everyone.

Dramatic Coastline

Often a sweeping highway, at other times a tortuously winding lane, the D010 road follows the Black Sea coast for hundreds of kilometres, offering an almost endless variety of views.

p485

Northeastern Anatolia

Ruins
Activities
Landscapes

Remote Outposts

Medieval Armenian and Georgian churches dot the steppe and valleys; isolated Ani was an Armenian capital and Silk Road trading centre. Near the Iranian border, mountainside İshak Paşa Palace is worthy of *One Thousand and One Nights*.

Outdoor Adventure

There are multiday trekking routes in the beautiful Kaçkar Mountains (Kaçkar Dağları), good-value skiing near Erzurum and Kars, and in February and March, the frozen expanse of Çıldır Gölü is a magical setting for horse-sleigh rides.

Upland Scenery

The east offers thrilling swathes of mountainscape from the Alpine landscapes of the Kaçkars, to wide, desolate moorlands around Kars and increasingly arid highlands further south.

p505

Southeastern Anatolia

History
Cuisine
Architecture

Ancient Remnants

The T-pillars of Göbeklitepe have turned a long-held archaeological theory on their head, Nemrut Dağı (Mt Nemrut) and its dramatic mountain surroundings are the location of the Commagene kingdom's ruins and Gaziantep's beautifully conceived museum showcases one of the world's most important mosaic collections.

Baklava Central

Gaziantep is revered as home to some of the world's best baklava. Join the Turkish tourists who descend en masse specifically to gorge on the city's famed sweet treats.

Church Relics

From the churches and monasteries scattered across the Tür Abdin to the intricately carved reliefs of Akdamar Kilisesi on Lake Van, the southeast is home to some of Turkey's most interesting Christian architecture.

p531

On the Road

İstanbul

POP 15.067 MILLION

Best Places to Eat

→ Antiochia (p128)

→ Çiya Sofrası (p130)

→ Hayvore (p127)

→ Mürver (p128)

→ Zübeyir Ocakbaşı (p127)

Best Places to Stay

→ Hotel Empress Zoe (p122)

→ Hotel Ibrahim Pasha (p122)

→ Hotel Alilass (p120)

→ Louis Appartements (p123)

→ Marmara Guesthouse (p120)

Why Go?

This magical meeting place of East and West has more top-drawer attractions than it has minarets (and that's a lot).

Here, you can visit Byzantine churches and Ottoman mosques in the morning, shop in chic boutiques during the afternoon and party at bars and clubs throughout the night. In the space of a few minutes you can hear the evocative strains of the call to prayer issuing from the Old City's tapering minarets, the sonorous horn of a crowded commuter ferry crossing between Europe and Asia, and the strident cries of a street hawker selling fresh seasonal produce. Put simply, this marvellous metropolis is an exercise in sensory seduction like no other.

Ask locals to describe what they love about İstanbul and they'll shrug, give a small smile and say merely that there is no other place like it. Spend a few days here, and you'll know exactly what they mean.

When to Go
İstanbul

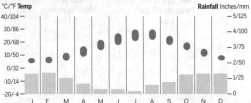

Apr Sunshine and balmy breezes usher in the colourful İstanbul Tulip Festival.

Jun & Jul Venues around town host high-profile jazz, classical and contemporary music festivals.

Oct Heat disperses and hotel prices drop. Pack an umbrella.

History

Byzantium

Legend tells us that the city of Byzantium was founded around 667 BC by a group of colonists from Megara, northwest of Athens. It was named after their leader, Byzas.

The new colony quickly prospered, largely due to its ability to levy tolls and harbour fees on ships passing through the Bosphorus, then as now an important waterway. A thriving marketplace was established and the inhabitants lived on traded goods and the abundant fish stocks in the surrounding waters.

In 512 BC Darius, emperor of Persia, captured the city during his campaign against the Scythians. Following the retreat of the Persians in 478 BC, the town came under the influence and protection of Athens and joined the Athenian League. Though this was a turbulent relationship, Byzantium stayed under Athenian rule until 355 BC, when it gained independence.

By the end of the Hellenistic period, Byzantium had formed an alliance with the Roman Empire. It retained its status as a free state, and kept this even after being officially incorporated into the Roman Empire in AD 79 by Vespasian. Life was relatively uneventful until the city's leaders made a big mistake: they picked the wrong side in a Roman war of succession following the death of Emperor Pertinax in AD 193. When Septimius Severus emerged victorious over his rival Pescennius Niger, he mounted a three-year siege of the city, eventually massacring Byzantium's citizens, razing its walls and burning it to the ground. Ancient Byzantium was no more.

The new emperor was aware of the city's important strategic position, and soon set about rebuilding it. He pardoned the remaining citizens and built a circuit of walls enclosing a city twice the size of its predecessor. The Hippodrome was built by Severus, as was a colonnaded way that followed the present path of Divan Yolu. Severus named his new city Augusta Antonina and it was subsequently ruled by a succession of emperors, including the great Diocletian (r 284–305).

Constantinople

Diocletian had decreed that after his retirement, the government of the Roman Empire should be overseen by co-emperors Galerius in the east (Augusta Antonina) and Constantine in the west (Rome). This resulted in a civil war, which was won by Constantine in AD 324 when he defeated Licinius, Galerius' successor, at Chrysopolis (the present-day suburb of Üsküdar).

With his victory, Constantine (r 324–37) became sole emperor of a reunited empire. He also became the first Christian emperor, though he didn't formally convert until he was on his deathbed.

Constantine also decided to move the capital of the empire to the shores of the Bosphorus, where he had forged his great victory and where the line between the Eastern and Western divisions of the empire had previously been drawn. He built a new, wider circle of walls around the site of Byzantium and laid out a magnificent city within. The Hippodrome was extended and a forum was built on the crest of the second hill, near today's Nuruosmaniye Mosque. The city was dedicated on 11 May 330 as New Rome, but soon came to be called Constantinople.

Constantinople continued to grow under the rule of the emperors. Theodosius I ('the Great'; r 379–95) had a forum built on the present site of Beyazıt Meydanı (Beyazıt Sq) and erected the Obelisk of Theodosius at the Hippodrome. His grandson Emperor Theodosius II (r 408–50), threatened by the forces of Attila the Hun, ordered that an even wider, more formidable circle of walls be built around the city. Encircling all seven hills of the city, the walls were completed in 413, only to be brought down by a series of earthquakes in 447. They were hastily rebuilt in a mere two months – the rapid approach of Attila and the Huns acting as a powerful stimulus. The Theodosian walls successfully held out invaders for the next 757 years and still stand today, though they are in an increasingly dilapidated state of repair.

Theodosius II died in 450 and was succeeded by a string of emperors, including the most famous of all Byzantine emperors, Justinian the Great. He further embellished Constantinople with great buildings, including SS Sergius and Bacchus, now known as Küçük (Little) Aya Sofya, Hagia Eirene (Aya İrini) and Hagia Sophia (Aya Sofya), which was completed in 537.

From 565 to 1025, a succession of warrior emperors kept invaders such as the Persians and the Avars at bay. Though the foreign armies often managed to get as far as Chalcedon (the present-day suburb of Kadıköy), none were able to breach Theodosius' land walls. The Arab armies of the nascent Islamic empire tried in 669, 674, 678 and 717-18, each time in vain.

In 1071 Emperor Romanus IV Diogenes (r 1068-71) led his army to eastern Anatolia to

continued on p80

İstanbul Highlights

1 Aya Sofya (p64) Marvelling at one of the world's truly great buildings.

2 Topkapı Palace (p72) Exploring this opulent palace.

3 Bosphorus Ferry Trip (p110) Journeying along this famed strait.

4 Grand Bazaar (p96) Getting lost amid the labyrinthine lanes.

5 Süleymaniye Mosque (p96) Admiring Süleyman the Magnificent's architectural legacy.

6 Basilica Cistern (p83) Heading underground into this cathedral-like space.

7 Beyoğlu (p127) Dining in the city's eating epicentre.

8 Kariye Mosque (p104) Gazing at magnificent examples of Byzantine art.

9 Blue Mosque (p70) Visiting the city's signature building.

10 Hamams (p117) Scrubbing-up in a historic hamam.

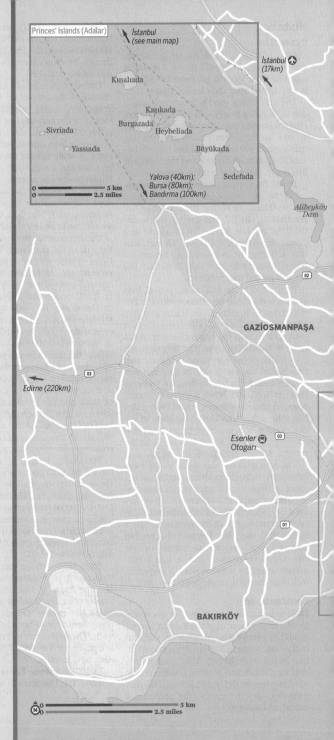

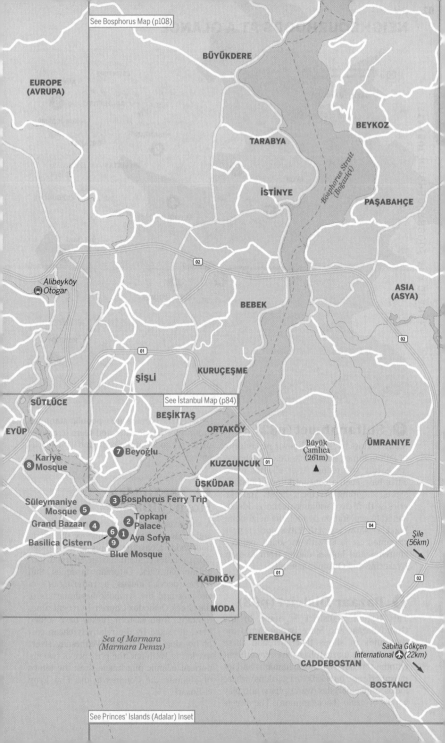

NEIGHBOURHOODS AT A GLANCE

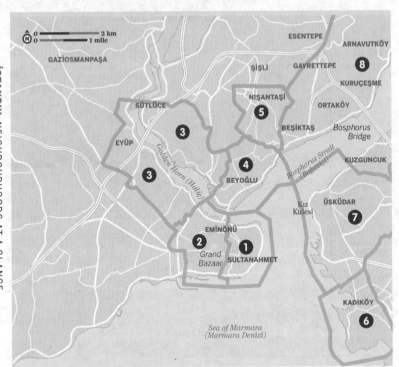

❶ Sultanahmet (p82)

Many visitors to İstanbul never make it out of Sultanahmet. And while this is a shame, it's hardly surprising. After all, not many cities have such a concentration of historic sights, shopping precincts, hotels and eateries within easy walking distance. Ideally suited to exploration by foot, the neighbourhood is a showcase of the city's glorious past, crammed as it is with mosques, palaces, churches and houses dating from Roman, Byzantine and Ottoman periods.

❷ Bazaar District (p93)

This beguiling district is home to the Grand Bazaar and Spice Bazaar. Amid the thousands of shops that surround these centuries-old marketplaces are magnificent Ottoman mosques, historic hamams and atmospheric *çay bahçesis* (tea gardens) where locals smoke nargiles (water pipes) and play games of *tavla* (backgammon). The streets between the bazaars are a popular stamping ground for İstanbullus, and seem to crackle with a good-humoured and infectious energy.

❸ The Golden Horn (p103)

A showcase of İstanbul's ethnically diverse and endlessly fascinating history, the neighbourhoods along the shores of the Golden Horn (Haliç) contain mosaic-adorned Byzantine churches, Ottoman mosques, Sufi *tekkes* (dervish lodges), a scattering of synagogues and the symbolic headquarters of the Greek Orthodox Church. In recent times migrants from eastern Turkey have settled here, attracted by the relatively cheap cost of housing, the vibrant Wednesday street market in Fatih and the presence of two important Islamic pilgrimage sites: the tombs of Mehmet the Conqueror and Ebu Eyüp el-Ensari.

taurants, high-end hotels and international fashion and design shops. Most of these are found in the streets surrounding the main artery, Teşvikiye Caddesi, prompting some locals to refer to that area as Teşvikiye. On weekend nights, the clubs in nearby Bomonti and Harbiye attract crowds from across the city.

❻ Kadıköy (p110)

In recent years locals have been decamping from the European side of town to Asia in ever-increasing numbers, setting up home in the suburbs that are strung south from the Bosphorus (Martyrs of July 15) Bridge. Of these, bustling Kadıköy and its annex Moda are of the most interest to visitors, being home to İstanbul's best produce market, great eateries, convivial cafes, world-class street art, grunge bars and a progressive vibe.

❼ Üsküdar (p111)

A working-class suburb with a conservative population, Üsküdar isn't blessed with the cafes, bars and restaurants that are in abundance in other city neighbourhoods, but it does have one very big asset – an array of magnificent imperial mosques. It offers a very different – and authentically local – experience to those travellers who choose to spend time here visiting these historic monuments.

❽ The Bosphorus Suburbs (p107)

Linking the Sea of Marmara (Marmara Denizi) with the Black Sea (Karadeniz), the Bosphorus Strait is the geographical spine of the city, and also its greatest treasure. Over the centuries it has been traversed by conquering armies, intrepid merchants and many an adventurous spirit. These days, thousands of İstanbullus commute along it; fishing vessels ply its waters; huge tankers and container ships make an occasionally dangerous progress down its central channel; and tourists ride the excursion ferries along its length. On one side is Europe, on the other Asia – both shores are lined with historic *yalıs* (seafront mansions).

❹ Beyoğlu (p99)

The high-octane hub of eating, drinking and entertainment in the city, Beyoğlu is where visitors and locals come in search of good restaurants and bars, live-music venues, hip hotels and edgy boutiques. Built around the major boulevard of İstiklal Caddesi, it incorporates a mix of bohemian residential districts such as Çukurcuma and Cihangir, bustling entertainment enclaves such as Asmalımescit, and historically rich pockets such as Galata and Karaköy that have morphed into entertainment epicentres.

❺ Nişantaşı, Bomonti & Harbiye (p133)

If you're a dab hand at air-kissing and striking a pose over a caffe latte, you'll feel totally at home in Nişantaşı. Serious shoppers, visiting celebs, PR professionals and the city's gilded youth gravitate towards this upmarket enclave, which is littered with bars, res-

TOP SIGHT
AYA SOFYA

There are many important monuments in İstanbul, but this venerable structure – commissioned by the great Byzantine emperor Justinian, consecrated as a church in 537, converted to a mosque by Mehmet the Conqueror in 1453 and declared a museum by Atatürk in 1935 and converted back into a mosque in 2020 – surpasses the rest due to its innovative architectural form, rich history, religious importance and extraordinary beauty.

Entering the Mosque

Enter the building and walk straight ahead through the outer and inner narthexes to reach the Imperial Door, which is crowned with a striking mosaic of Christ as Pantocrator (Ruler of All). Christ holds a book that carries the inscription 'Peace be With You. I am the Light of the World.' At his feet an emperor (probably Leo VI) prostrates himself. The Virgin Mary is on Christ's left and to his right is the Archangel Gabriel.

Through the Imperial Door is the building's main space, now its prayer hall, famous for its dome, huge nave and gold mosaics.

Nave

Made 'transparent' by its profusion of windows and columned arcades, Aya Sofya's nave (now prayer hall) is as visually arresting as it is enormous.

The chandeliers hanging low above the floor are Ottoman additions. In Byzantine times, rows of glass oil lamps

DON'T MISS

➡ Cover shoulders and knees.

➡ Women should don a headscarf.

➡ Leave shoes at the entrance to the inner narthex.

➡ If non-Muslim, don't enter during prayer time.

➡ Check prayer times at https://namazvakitleri.diyanet.gov.tr/en-US.

PRACTICALITIES

➡ Hagia Sophia, Ayasofya-i Kebir Cami-i Şerifi

➡ Map p88

➡ ☎ 0212-522 1750

➡ https://muze.gen.tr/muze-detay/ayasofya

➡ Aya Sofya Meydanı 1

➡ Closed during prayer times

➡ 🚇 Sultanahmet

lined the balustrades of the gallery and the walkway at the base of the dome.

The focal point at this level is the apse. The magnificent 9th-century mosaic of the Virgin and Christ Child is now obscured by curtains even outside of prayer times. The minber (pulpit) and the mihrab (prayer niche indicating the direction of Mecca) were added during the Ottoman period. The mosaics above the apse once depicted the archangels Gabriel and Michael; today only fragments remain.

The Byzantine emperors were crowned while seated on a throne placed within the omphalion, the section of inlaid marble in the main floor. The ornate library behind the omphalion was built by Sultan Mahmut I in 1739.

The large 19th-century medallions inscribed with gilt Arabic letters are the work of master calligrapher Mustafa İzzet Efendi, and give the names of God (Allah), Mohammed and the early caliphs Ali and Abu Bakr.

The curious elevated kiosk screened from public view is the imperial loge (hünkar mahfili). Sultan Abdül Mecit I had this built in 1848 so he could enter, pray and leave unseen, thus preserving the imperial mystique.

Looking up towards the northeast (to your left if you are facing the apse), you should be able to see three mosaics at the base of the northern tympanum (semicircle) beneath the dome. These are 9th-century portraits of St Ignatius the Younger, St John Chrysostom and St Ignatius Theodorus of Antioch. To their right, on one of the pendentives (concave triangular segments below the dome), is a 14th-century mosaic of the face of a seraph (six-winged angel charged with caretaking God's throne).

In the side aisle at the bottom of the ramp to the upstairs galleries is a column with a worn copper facing pierced by a hole. According to legend, the pillar, known as the Weeping Column, was blessed by St Gregory the Miracle Worker and putting one's finger into the hole is said to lead to ailments being healed if the finger emerges moist.

Dome

Aya Sofya's dome is 30m in diameter and 56m in height. It's supported by 40 massive ribs constructed of special hollow bricks, and these ribs rest on four huge pillars concealed in the interior walls. On its completion, the Byzantine historian Procopius described it as being 'hung from heaven on a golden chain', and it's easy to see why. The great Ottoman architect Mimar Sinan, who spent his entire professional life trying to design a mosque to match

---

AYA SOFYA HISTORY

Known as Hagia Sophia in Greek, Sancta Sophia in Latin and the Church of the Divine Wisdom in English, Aya Sofya has a history that's as long as it is fascinating. It was constructed on the site of Byzantium's acropolis, which was also the site of two earlier churches of the same name, one destroyed by fire and another during the Nika riots of AD 532. On entering his commission for the first time, Justinian exclaimed, 'Glory to God that I have been judged worthy of such a work. Oh Solomon! I have outdone you!' Entering the building today, his hubris is understandable. The less impressive exterior offers little preparation for the sublimely beautiful interior, with its magnificent domed roof soaring heavenward.

Vikings are said to have left the 'Eric woz here'–type graffiti that is carved into the balustrade in the upstairs south gallery. You'll find it near the *Deesis* mosaic.

the magnificence and beauty of Aya Sofya, used the same trick of concealing pillars and 'floating' the dome when designing the Süleymaniye Mosque almost 1000 years later.

Upstairs Galleries

The Aya Sofya's upstairs galleries are currently closed for restoration. When open again, access them by walking up the switchback ramp at the northern end of the inner narthex. In the south gallery (straight ahead and then left through the 6th-century marble door) are the remnants of a magnificent **Deesis** (Last Judgement). This 13th-century mosaic depicts Christ with the Virgin Mary on his left and John the Baptist on his right.

Close by is the **Tomb of Enrico Dandolo**, a blind Venetian doge who led the Sack of Constantinople during the Fourth Crusade (1202–04) and died soon afterwards. The marker was laid in the 19th century by an Italian restoration team, the original having been destroyed by the Ottomans.

Further on, at the eastern (apse) end of the gallery, is an 11th-century mosaic depicting **Christ Enthroned with Empress Zoe and Constantine IX Monomachos**.

To the right of Zoe and Constantine is a 12th-century mosaic depicting the **Virgin Mary, Emperor John Comnenus II and Empress Eirene**. The emperor, who was known as 'John the Good', is on the Virgin's left and the empress, who was known for her charitable works, is to her right; both are giving money to Aya Sofya. Their son **Alexios** is depicted next to Eirene; he died soon after this portrait was made. Eirene's stone sarcophagus is downstairs in the outer narthex.

Outbuildings

Exit the inner narthex through the **Beautiful Gate**, a magnificent bronze gate dating from the 2nd century BC. This originally adorned a pagan temple in Tarsus

AYA SOFYA

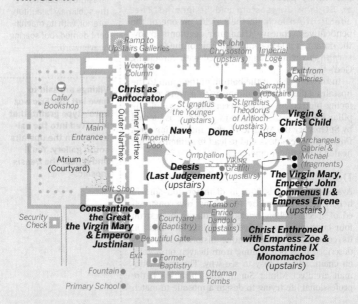

Aya Sofya's dome (p65)

THE BUTTRESSES

The original building form designed by Aya Sofya's architects, Anthemios of Tralles and Isidoros of Miletus, has been compromised by the addition of 24 buttresses, added to reinforce the building and its enormous dome. Some date from Byzantine times, others from the Ottoman period; seven buttresses are on the eastern side of the building, four on the southern, four on the northern and five on the western. The remaining four support the structure as weight towers.

and was brought to İstanbul by Emperor Theophilos in 838.

As you reach the gate, be sure to look back to admire the 10th-century mosaic of **Constantine the Great, the Virgin Mary and the Emperor Justinian** on the lunette of the inner doorway. Constantine (right) is offering the Virgin, who holds the Christ Child, the city of İstanbul; Justinian (left) is offering her Aya Sofya.

The doorway to your left just after the Beautiful Gate leads into a small courtyard that was once part of a 6th-century **baptistry**. In the 17th century the baptistry was converted into a tomb for Sultans Mustafa I and İbrahim I. The huge stone basin displayed in the courtyard is the original **font**.

To the right after you exit the main building is a recently restored rococo-style *şadırvan* (ablutions fountain) dating from 1740. Next to it is a small *sibyan maktab* (primary school) also dating from 1740. The small structure next to the gate is the *muvakkithane* (place where prayer hours were determined), built in 1853.

The first of Aya Sofya's minarets was added by order of Mehmet the Conqueror. Sinan designed the other three between 1574 and 1576.

After exiting the museum grounds, walk east (left) and turn left again on Babıhümayun Caddesi to visit the **Aya Sofya Tombs** (Aya Sofya Müzesi Padişah Türbeleri; Map p88; ☻9am-6pm Apr-Oct, to 5pm Nov-Mar) **FREE**.

The last Byzantine emperor, Constantine XI, prayed in Aya Sofya just before midnight on 28 May 1453. Hours later he was killed while defending the city walls from the attack being staged by the army of Mehmet II. The city fell to the Ottomans on the 29th, and Mehmet's first act of victory was to make his way to Aya Sofya and declare that it should immediately be converted to a mosque.

Aya Sofya

A TIMELINE

537 Emperor Justinian, depicted in one of the church's famous ❶ mosaics, presides over the consecration of Byzantium's new basilica, Hagia Sophia (Church of the Holy Wisdom).

557 The huge ❷ dome, damaged during an earthquake, collapses and is rebuilt.

843 The second Byzantine Iconoclastic period ends and figurative ❸ mosaics begin to be added to the interior. These include a depiction of the Empress Zoe and her third husband, Emperor Constantine IX Monomachos.

1204 Soldiers of the Fourth Crusade led by the Doge of Venice, Enrico Dandolo, conquer and ransack Constantinople. Dandolo's ❹ tomb is eventually erected in the church whose desecration he presided over.

1453 The city falls to the Ottomans; Mehmet II orders that Hagia Sophia be converted to a mosque and renamed Aya Sofya.

1577 Sultan Selim II is buried in a specially designed tomb, which sits alongside the ❺ tombs of four other Ottoman Sultans in Aya Sofya's grounds.

1847–49 Sultan Abdül Mecit I orders that the building be restored and redecorated; the huge ❻ Ottoman Medallions in the nave are added.

1935 The mosque is converted into a museum by order of Mustafa Kemal Atatürk, president of the new Turkish Republic.

2009 The face of one of the four ❼ seraphs is uncovered during major restoration works in the nave.

2012 Restoration of the exterior walls and western upper gallery commences.

TOP TIP

Bring binoculars if you want to properly view the mosaic portraits in the apse and under the dome.

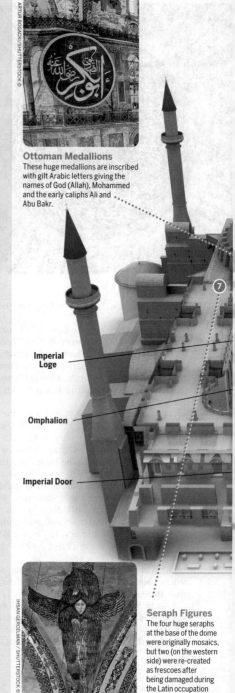

ARTUR BOGACKI/SHUTTERSTOCK ©

Ottoman Medallions
These huge medallions are inscribed with gilt Arabic letters giving the names of God (Allah), Mohammed and the early caliphs Ali and Abu Bakr.

Imperial Loge

Omphalion

Imperial Door

IHSAN GERCELMAN / SHUTTERSTOCK ©

Seraph Figures
The four huge seraphs at the base of the dome were originally mosaics, but two (on the western side) were re-created as frescoes after being damaged during the Latin occupation (1204–61).

Dome

Soaring 56m from ground level, the dome was originally covered in gold mosaics but was decorated with calligraphy during the 1847–49 restoration works overseen by Swiss-born architects Gaspard and Giuseppe Fossati.

Christ Enthroned with Empress Zoe and Constantine IX Monomachos

This mosaic portrait in the upper gallery depicts Zoe, one of only three Byzantine women to rule as empress in their own right.

Ottoman Tombs

The tombs of five Ottoman sultans and their families are located in Aya Sofya's southern corner and can be accessed via Babıhümayun Caddesi. One of these occupies the church's original Baptistry.

Aya Sofya Tombs

Former Baptistry

Muvakkithane
(place where prayer hours were determined)

Main Entrance

Exit

Ablutions Fountain

Primary School

Grave of Enrico Dandolo

The Venetian doge died in 1205, only one year after he and his Crusaders had stormed the city. A 19th-century marker in the upper gallery indicates the probable location of his grave.

Constantine the Great, the Virgin Mary and Emperor Justinian

This 11th-century mosaic shows Constantine (right) offering the Virgin Mary the city of Constantinople. Justinian (left) is offering her Hagia Sophia.

TOP SIGHT
BLUE MOSQUE

İstanbul's most photogenic building was the grand project of Sultan Ahmet I (r 1603–17), whose *türbe* (tomb) is located on the north side of the site facing Sultanahmet Park. Officially known as the Sultanahmet Camii (Sultanahmet Mosque), its wonderfully curvaceous exterior features a cascade of domes and six slender minarets, while blue İznik tiles adorn the interior and give the building its unofficial but commonly used name.

The Exterior

Ahmet set out to build a monument that would rival and even surpass the nearby Aya Sofya in grandeur and beauty. Indeed, the young sultan was so enthusiastic about the project that he is said to have worked with the labourers and craftsmen on site, pushing them along and rewarding extra effort. Ahmet did in fact come close to his goal of rivalling Aya Sofya – and in so doing he made future generations of local hoteliers happy: a 'Blue Mosque view' from the roof terrace is a top selling point of hotels in the area.

With the mosque's exterior, the architect, Sedefkâr Mehmet Ağa, managed to orchestrate a visual wham-bam effect similar to that of Aya Sofya's interior. Its curves are voluptuous; its courtyard is the biggest of all the Ottoman mosques; and when built it had more minarets than any other İstanbul mosque – a record only recently equalled by the colossal new Çamlıca Mosque on the city's Asian side. In fact, there was concern at the time of the Blue Mosque's construction that the sultan was being presumptuous in specifying six minarets, as the only equivalent was in Mecca.

In order to fully appreciate the mosque's design you should approach it via the middle of the Hippodrome rather than entering from Sultanahmet Park. When inside the courtyard,

DON'T MISS

→ The approach from the Hippodrome

→ The İznik tiles

→ The carved white marble *minber*

PRACTICALITIES

→ Sultanahmet Camii

→ Map p88

→ ☑ 0212-458 4468

→ Hippodrome

→ ☉ closed to non-worshippers during 6 daily prayer times & on Fri mornings

→ 🚇 Sultanahmet

which is the same size as the mosque's interior, you'll be able to appreciate the perfect proportions of the building. Walk towards the mosque through the gate in the peripheral wall, noting on the way the small dome atop the next gate: this is the motif Sedefkâr Mehmet Ağa uses to lift your eyes to heaven. As you cross the outer courtyard, your eyes follow a flight of stairs up to yet more domes: that of the ablutions fountain in the centre of the mosque courtyard and, as you ascend the stairs, a semidome over the mosque's main door, then one above it, and another and another. Finally the main dome crowns the whole, and your attention is drawn to the sides, where forests of smaller domes reinforce the effect, completed by the minarets, which lift your eyes heavenward.

The Interior

The mosque is such a popular tourist sight that admission is controlled in order to preserve its sacred atmosphere. Only worshippers are admitted through the main door; visitors must use the south door (follow the signs) and remove their shoes.

The interior is conceived on a grand scale: it features more than 21,000 İznik tiles, 260 windows and a huge central prayer space. The **stained-glass windows** and **İznik tiles** immediately attract attention. Though the windows are replacements, they still create the luminous effect of the originals, which came from Venice. Tiles line the walls with an explosion of flower motifs, particularly in the upstairs galleries (which are not open to the public).

Once inside, it's easy to see that the mosque, which was constructed between 1606 and 1616, more than 1000 years after nearby Aya Sofya, is not as architecturally daring as its predecessor. Four massive pillars hold up the less ambitious dome, a sturdier solution lacking the innovation and grace of the 'floating' dome in Justinian's cathedral.

The semidomes and the dome are painted with graceful **arabesques**. Of note in the main space are the **müezzin mahfili** (*müezzin's* lodge), a raised platform where the *müezzin* repeats the call to prayer at the start of each service; the **mihrab** (niche indicating the direction of Mecca), which features a piece of the sacred Black Stone from the Kaaba in Mecca; and the high, elaborate **kursi** (chair) from which the imam gives the sermon on Fridays. The beautifully carved white marble **minber** (pulpit), with its curtained doorway at floor level, features a flight of steps and a small kiosk topped by a spire.

SULTAN AHMET I

Designed by Sedefkâr Mehmet Ağa and built in 1617–19, Ahmet I's *türbe* (tomb) is on the north side of the mosque facing Sultanahmet Park. Ahmet, who had ascended the imperial throne aged 13, died at just 27, one year after construction of the mosque was completed. Buried with him are his wife, Kösem (strangled to death in the Topkapı Harem), and his sons, Sultan Osman II (r 1618–22), Sultan Murat IV (r 1623–40) and Prince Beyazıt (murdered by order of Murat). Like the mosque, the *türbe* features fine İznik tiles.

Mosques built by the great and powerful usually included numerous public-service institutions, including hospitals, soup kitchens and schools. Here, a large *medrese* (Islamic school of higher studies) on the northwestern side of the complex (closed to the public) and *arasta* (row of shops by a mosque; now the Arasta Bazaar; p91) remain.

TOP SIGHT
TOPKAPI PALACE

Topkapı Palace is the subject of more colourful stories than most of the world's museums put together. Libidinous sultans, ambitious courtiers, beautiful concubines and scheming eunuchs lived and worked here between the 15th and 19th centuries when it was the court of the Ottoman Empire. Visiting its opulent pavilions, jewel-filled Treasury and sprawling Harem gives a fascinating glimpse into their lives.

First Court

Before you enter the Imperial Gate (cnr Babıhümayun Caddesi & Soğukçeşme Sokak) of Topkapı, take a look at the ornate structure in the cobbled square just outside. This is the rococo-style Fountain of Sultan Ahmet III (Babıhümayun Caddesi), built in 1728. As you pass through the Imperial Gate, you enter the First Court, known as the Court of the Janissaries or the Parade Court. On your left is the Byzantine church of Hagia Eirene, more commonly known as Aya İrini (Hagia Eirene, Church of the Divine Peace; adult/child under 8yr ₺36/free).

Second Court

The Middle Gate (Ortakapı or Bab-üs Selâm) led to the palace's Second Court, used for the business of running the empire.

The great Palace Kitchens (Matbah-ı Âmire) on the right (east) incorporate the Helvahane, a dedicated section where confectionary was made.

DON'T MISS

➡ Imperial Council Chamber

➡ Harem

➡ Audience Chamber

➡ Marble Terrace

➡ Sacred Safekeeping Rooms

PRACTICALITIES

➡ Topkapı Sarayı

➡ Map p88

➡ 📞 0212-512 0480

➡ www.topkapisarayi.gov.tr

➡ Babıhümayun Caddesi

➡ palace adult/child under 8yr ₺72/free, Harem adult/child under 6yr ₺42/free, audio guide palace/harem/both ₺20/20/30

➡ ⊘ 9am-6.45pm Wed-Mon Apr-Sep, to 4.45pm Oct-Mar, last entry 45min before closing

➡ 🚇 Sultanahmet

On the left (west) side of the Second Court is the ornate Imperial Council Chamber (Dîvân-ı Hümâyûn). The council met here to discuss matters of state, and the sultan sometimes eavesdropped through the gold grille high in the wall.

North of the Imperial Council Chamber is the Outer Treasury, where an impressive collection of Ottoman and European arms and armour is displayed, including a 14th-century Hungarian sword fit for a giant.

Harem

The entrance to the Harem is beneath the Tower of Justice on the western side of the Second Court. If you decide to visit – and we highly recommend that you do – you'll need to buy a dedicated ticket. The visitor route through the Harem changes when rooms are closed for restoration, so some of the areas mentioned here may not be open during your visit.

As popular belief would have it, the Harem was a place where the sultan could engage in debauchery at will. In more prosaic reality, these were the imperial family quarters, and every detail of Harem life was governed by tradition, obligation and ceremony. The word 'harem' literally means 'forbidden' or 'private'.

The Harem complex has six floors, but only one of these can be visited. This is approached via the Carriage Gate. Next to the gate is the Dormitory of the Corps of the Palace Guards, a meticulously restored two-storey structure featuring swathes of 16th- and 17th-century İznik tiles. It once housed members of the palace guard. Inside the gate is the Dome with Cupboards, the Harem treasury where financial records were kept. Beyond it is a room where the Harem's eunuch guards were stationed. Beyond it is the Hall with the Fountain, lined with fine Kütahya tiles from the 17th century and home to a marble horse-mounting block once used by the sultans. Adjoining this is the Mosque of the Black Eunuchs, which features depictions of Mecca on its 17th-century tiles.

Beyond is the Courtyard of the Black Eunuchs, also decorated with Kütahya tiles. Behind the marble colonnade on the left are the Black Eunuchs' Dormitories. As many as 200 lived here, guarding the doors and waiting on the women of the Harem.

At the far end of the courtyard is the Main Gate into the Harem, as well as a guard room featuring two gigantic gilded mirrors. On the left, the Concubines' Corridor, with frescoes of the palace at the far end, leads to the Courtyard of the Concubines and Sultan's Consorts. This is surrounded by baths, a laundry fountain, dormitories and private apartments.

WOMEN OF THE HAREM

Islam forbade enslaving Muslims, so the concubines in Topkapı's Harem were foreigners or infidels. Girls were bought as slaves or were received as gifts from nobles and potentates. Many of the girls were from Eastern Europe and all were noted for their beauty. The most famous was Haseki Hürrem (Joyous One), more commonly known as Roxelana, who was the consort of Süleyman the Magnificent. The daughter of a Ruthenian (Ukrainian) Orthodox priest, she was captured by Crimean Tatars, who brought her to Constantinople to be sold in the slave market.

The sultans supported as many as 300 concubines in the Harem, although numbers were usually lower than this. Upon entering the Harem, the girls would be schooled in Islam and in Turkish culture and language, as well as the arts of make-up, dress, comportment, music, reading, writing, embroidery and dancing. They then entered a meritocracy, first as ladies-in-waiting to the sultan's concubines and children, then to the sultan's mother and finally – if they were particularly attractive and talented – to the sultan himself.

TOPKAPI PALACE (TOPKAPI SARAYİ)

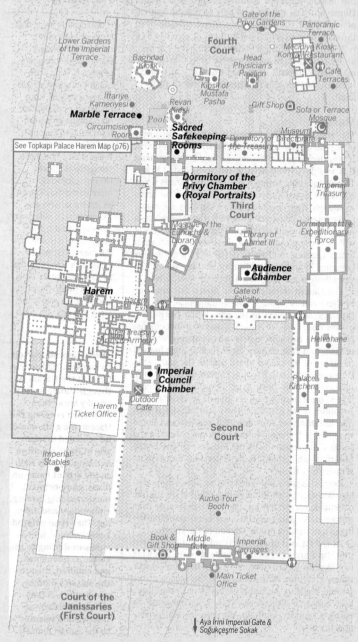

Gate of the
Privy Gardens

Panoramic
Terrace

**Fourth
Court**

Lower Gardens
of the Imperial
Terrace

Baghdad
Kiosk

Mecidiye Kiosk;
Konyalı Restaurant

Head
Physician's
Pavilion

Café
Terraces

İftariye
Kameriyesi

Kiosk of
Mustafa
Pasha

Marble Terrace

Revan
Kiosk

Pool

Gift Shop

Sofa or Terrace
Mosque

Circumcision
Room

**Sacred
Safekeeping
Rooms**

Dormitory of
the Treasury

Museum

Dormitory of Directorate

See Topkapı Palace Harem Map (p76)

**Dormitory of the
Privy Chamber
(Royal Portraits)**

Imperial
Treasury

**Third
Court**

Dormitory of the
Expeditionary
Force

Mosque of the
Eunuchs &
Library

Library of
Ahmet III

**Audience
Chamber**

Harem

Gate of
Felicity

Harem
Exit

Helvahane

Outer Treasury
(Arms & Armour)

**Imperial
Council
Chamber**

Palace
Kitchens

Outdoor
Café

Harem
Ticket Office

**Second
Court**

Imperial
Stables

Audio Tour
Booth

Book &
Gift Shop

Middle
Gate

Imperial
Carriages

Main Ticket
Office

**Court of the
Janissaries
(First Court)**

↓ Aya İrini Imperial Gate &
↓ Soğukçeşme Sokak

Turn right at the end of the Concubines' Corridor for a room decorated with a tiled chimney, followed by the **Apartments of the Valide Sultan**, the centre of power in the Harem. From these ornate rooms the *valide sultan* (mother of the reigning sultan) oversaw and controlled her huge 'family'.

Past the **Courtyard of the Valide Sultan** is a splendid reception room with a large fireplace that leads to a vestibule covered in Kütahya and İznik tiles dating from the 17th century. This is where the princes, *valide sultan* and senior concubines waited before entering the **Imperial Hall** for an audience with the sultan.

Nearby is the **Privy Chamber of Murat III**, one of the most sumptuous rooms in the palace. The restored three-tiered marble fountain was designed to give the sound of cascading water and to make it difficult to eavesdrop on the sultan's conversations.

Continue to the **Privy Chamber of Ahmet III** and peek into the adjoining **dining room** built in 1705. The latter is lined with wooden panels decorated with images of flowers and fruits.

Back through the Privy Chamber of Murat III are two of the most beautiful rooms in the Harem – the **Twin Kiosk/Apartments of the Crown Prince**. These two rooms date from around 1600; note the painted canvas dome in the first room.

Past these rooms is the **Courtyard of the Favourites**. Over the edge of the courtyard (really a terrace) you'll see a large empty pool. Overlooking the courtyard are the tiny windows of the many small dark rooms comprising the *kafes* (cage) where brothers or sons of the sultan were imprisoned. Adjoining it is the tiled **Harem Mosque** with its baroque *mihrab* (niche indicating the direction of Mecca).

From here, visitors follow the passage known as the Golden Road and exit into the palace's Third Court.

Third Court

The Third Court is entered through the **Gate of Felicity**. The sultan's private domain, it was staffed and guarded by white eunuchs. Inside is the **Audience Chamber**. Important officials and foreign ambassadors were brought to this little kiosk to conduct the high business of state.

Right behind the Audience Chamber is the **Library of Ahmet III**, built in 1719.

On the eastern edge of the Third Court is the **Dormitory of the Expeditionary Force**, which was closed for restoration at the time of research. When it reopens it will house the palace's rich collection of imperial robes, kaftans and uniforms worked in silver and gold thread. On the other side of the Third Court

MEHMET THE CONQUEROR

Mehmet the Conqueror had built the first stage of the palace shortly after the Conquest in 1453, and lived in the compound behind the Imperial Gate until his death in 1481. The Ottoman sultans continued to live in Topkapı's rarefied environment until the 19th century, when they moved to ostentatious European-style palaces such as Dolmabahçe and Çırağan.

Palace overload? Stop in to Cafer-ağa Medresesi Çay Bahçesi (p130) for a refreshing çay or juice in the atmospheric courtyard.

TOPKAPI PALACE HAREM

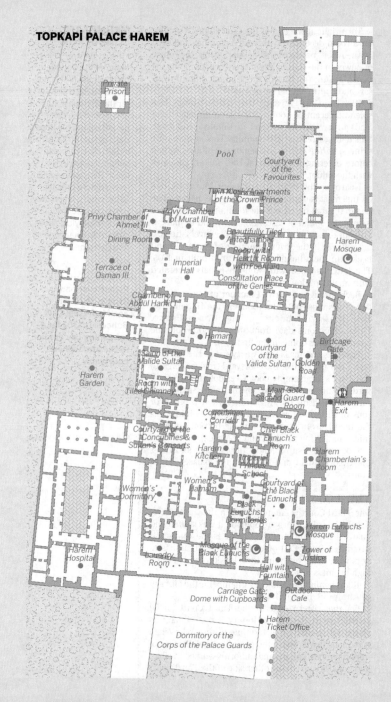

Private Prison

Pool

Courtyard of the Favourites

Tulip Kiosk Apartments of the Crown Prince

Privy Chamber of Ahmet III

Privy Chamber of Murat III

Dining Room

Beautifully Tiled Antechamber

Room with Hearth

Room with Pool Atrium

Harem Mosque

Terrace of Osman III

Imperial Hall

Consultation Place of the Genies

Chamber of Abdül Hamit I

Hamam

Courtyard of the Valide Sultan

Birdcage Gate

Salon of the Valide Sultan

Golden Road

Harem Garden

Room with Tiled Chimney

Main Gate; Second Guard Room

Harem Exit

Concubines' Corridor

Courtyard of the Concubines & Sultan's Consorts

Chief Black Eunuch's Room

Harem Kitchen

Harem Chamberlain's Room

Princes' School

Women's Hamam

Courtyard of the Black Eunuchs

Women's Dormitory

Black Eunuchs' Dormitories

Harem Hospital

Mosque of the Black Eunuchs

Harem Eunuchs' Mosque

Laundry Room

Tower of Justice

Hall with Fountain

Carriage Gate; Dome with Cupboards

Outdoor Cafe

Harem Ticket Office

Dormitory of the Corps of the Palace Guards

are the **Sacred Safekeeping Rooms**. These rooms house many relics of the Prophet. An imam sometimes sits near the exit and recites from the Koran.

Next to the Sacred Safekeeping Rooms is the **Dormitory of the Privy Chamber**, which houses portraits of 36 sultans. The highlight is Konstantin Kapidagli's painting of the **Enthronement Ceremony of Sultan Selim III** (1789) with its curving line of turbaned spectators.

En route to the Fourth Court you will pass the **Dormitory of the Treasury**, which accommodated the palace treasury's many staff, who numbered over 150 by the 18th century.

Imperial Treasury

Located on the eastern edge of the Third Court, Topkapı's Treasury features an incredible collection of objects made from or decorated with gold, silver, rubies, emeralds, jade, pearls and diamonds. The building itself was constructed during Mehmet the Conqueror's reign in 1460 and was used originally as reception rooms. It was closed for a major restoration when we last visited.

Fourth Court

Pleasure pavilions occupy the palace's Fourth Court, also known as the Tulip Garden. These include the **Mecidiye Kiosk**, which was built by Abdül Mecit (r 1839–61) according to 19th-century European models.

Up steps from the Mecidiye Kiosk is the **Head Physician's Pavilion**. Interestingly, the head physician was always one of the sultan's Jewish subjects. On this terrace you will also find the late-17th-century **Kiosk of Kara Mustafa Pasha** (Sofa Köşkü), with its gilded ceiling, painted walls and delicate stained-glass windows. Up the stairs at the end of the Tulip Garden is the **Marble Terrace**, a platform with a decorative pool, three pavilions and the whimsical **İftariye Kameriyesi**, a small structure commissioned by İbrahim I in 1640 as a picturesque place to break the fast of Ramazan.

Murat IV built the **Revan Kiosk** in 1636 after reclaiming the city of Yerevan (now in Armenia) from Persia. The kiosk was also known as the Chamber of Turbans (Sarık Odası) because the sultans' turbans were kept there. In 1639 Murat IV constructed the **Baghdad Kiosk**, one of the last examples of classical palace architecture, to commemorate his victory over that city. Notice its superb İznik tiles, painted ceiling and mother-of-pearl and tortoiseshell inlay. The small **Circumcision Room** (Sünnet Odası) was used for the ritual that admits Muslim boys to manhood. Built by İbrahim in 1640, the outer walls of the chamber are graced by particularly beautiful tile panels.

IMPERIAL TREASURY

When the Imperial Treasury reopens, look out for the jewel-encrusted Sword of Süleyman the Magnificent and the extraordinary Throne of Ahmed I (aka Arife Throne), which is inlaid with mother-of-pearl and was designed by Sedefkâr Mehmet Ağa, architect of the Blue Mosque. And don't miss the Treasury's famous Topkapı Dagger, object of the criminal heist in Jules Dassin's 1964 film *Topkapı*. This features three enormous emeralds on the hilt and a watch set into the pommel. Also worth seeking out is the Kasıkçı (Spoonmaker's) Diamond, a teardrop-shaped 86-carat rock surrounded by dozens of smaller stones that was first worn by Mehmet IV at his accession to the throne in 1648.

Topkapı Palace

DAILY LIFE IN THE IMPERIAL COURT

A visit to this opulent palace compound, with its courtyards, harem and pavilions, offers a fascinating glimpse into the lives of the Ottoman sultans. During its heyday, royal wives and children, concubines, eunuchs and servants were among the 4000 people living within Topkapı's walls.

The sultans and their families rarely left the palace grounds, relying on courtiers and diplomats to bring them news of the outside world. Most visitors would go straight to the magnificent **1 Imperial Council Chamber**, where the sultan's grand vizier and Dîvân (Council) regularly met to discuss affairs of state and receive foreign dignitaries. Many of these visitors brought lavish gifts and tributes to embellish the **2 Imperial Treasury**.

After receiving any guests and meeting with the Dîvân, the grand vizier would make his way through the ornate **3 Gate of Felicity** into the Third Court, the palace's residential quarter. Here, he would brief the sultan on the deliberations and decisions of the Dîvân in the colonnaded **4 Audience Chamber**.

Meanwhile, day-to-day domestic chores and intrigues would be underway in the **5 Harem** and servants would be preparing feasts in the massive **6 Palace Kitchens**. Amid all this activity, the **7 Marble Terrace** was a tranquil retreat where the sultan would come to relax, look out over the city and perhaps regret his sequestered lifestyle.

Harem
The sultan, his mother and the crown prince had sumptuously decorated private apartments in the Harem. The most beautiful of these are the Twin Kiosks (pictured), which were used by the crown prince.

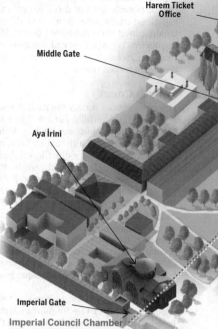

Harem Ticket Office

Middle Gate

Aya İrini

Imperial Gate

Imperial Council Chamber
This is where the Dîvân (Council) made laws, citizens presented petitions and foreign dignitaries were presented to the court. The sultan sometimes eavesdropped on proceedings through the window with the golden grille.

DON'T MISS

There are spectacular views from the terrace above the Konyalı Restaurant and also from the Marble Terrace in the Fourth Court.

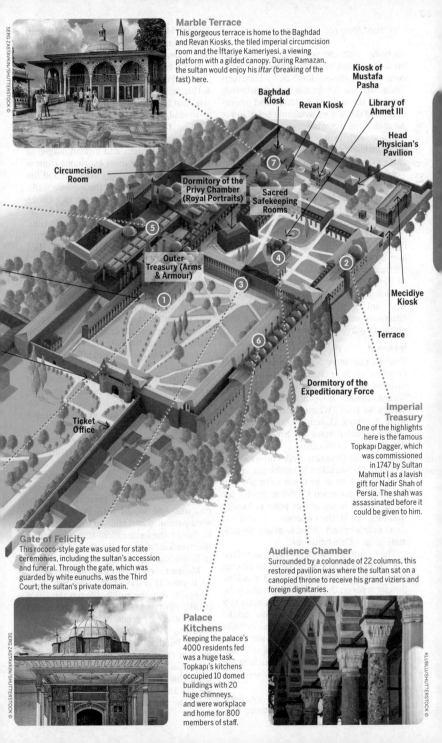

Marble Terrace
This gorgeous terrace is home to the Baghdad and Revan Kiosks, the tiled imperial circumcision room and the İftariye Kameriyesi, a viewing platform with a gilded canopy. During Ramazan, the sultan would enjoy his *iftar* (breaking of the fast) here.

Kiosk of Mustafa Pasha

Baghdad Kiosk

Revan Kiosk

Library of Ahmet III

Head Physician's Pavilion

Circumcision Room

Dormitory of the Privy Chamber (Royal Portraits)

Sacred Safekeeping Rooms

(7)

(5)

Outer Treasury (Arms & Armour)

(1)

(3)

(4)

(2)

Mecidiye Kiosk

Terrace

(6)

Dormitory of the Expeditionary Force

Imperial Treasury
One of the highlights here is the famous Topkapı Dagger, which was commissioned in 1747 by Sultan Mahmut I as a lavish gift for Nadir Shah of Persia. The shah was assassinated before it could be given to him.

Ticket Office

Gate of Felicity
This rococo-style gate was used for state ceremonies, including the sultan's accession and funeral. Through the gate, which was guarded by white eunuchs, was the Third Court, the sultan's private domain.

Audience Chamber
Surrounded by a colonnade of 22 columns, this restored pavilion was where the sultan sat on a canopied throne to receive his grand viziers and foreign dignitaries.

Palace Kitchens
Keeping the palace's 4000 residents fed was a huge task. Topkapı's kitchens occupied 10 domed buildings with 20 huge chimneys, and were workplace and home for 800 members of staff.

SERG ZASTAVKIN/SHUTTERSTOCK ©

SERG ZASTAVKIN/SHUTTERSTOCK ©

KLUBLU/SHUTTERSTOCK ©

continued from p59

do battle with the Seljuk Turks, who had been forced out of Central Asia by the encroaching Mongols. However, at Manzikert (Malazgirt) the Byzantines were disastrously defeated, the emperor captured and imprisoned, and the former Byzantine heartland of Anatolia thus thrown open to Turkish invasion and settlement.

As Turkish power was consolidated to the east of Constantinople, the power of Venice – always a maritime and commercial rival to Constantinople – grew in the West. This coincided with the launch of the First Crusade and the arrival in Constantinople of the first of the Crusaders in 1096.

In 1204 soldiers of the Fourth Crusade led by Enrico Dandolo, Doge of Venice, attacked and ransacked the city. They then ruled it with an ally, Count Baldwin of Flanders, until 1261, when soldiers under Michael VIII Palaiologos, a Byzantine aristocrat in exile who had risen to become co-emperor of Nicaea, successfully recaptured it. The Byzantine Empire was restored.

İstanbul

Two decades after Michael VIII reclaimed Constantinople, a Turkish warlord named Ertuğrul died in the village of Söğüt near Nicaea. He left his son Osman, who was known as Gazi (Warrior for the Faith), a small territory. Osman's followers became known in the Empire as Osmanlıs and in the West as the Ottomans.

By 1440 the Ottoman armies under Murat II (r 1421–51) had taken Thessalonica, unsuccessfully laid siege to Constantinople and Belgrade, and battled Christian armies in Transylvania. It was at this point in history that Mehmet II 'the Conqueror' (r 1451–81) came to power and vowed to attain the ultimate prize – Constantinople.

The Byzantines had closed the mouth of the Golden Horn with a heavy chain to prevent Ottoman boats from sailing in and attacking the city walls on the northern side. Not to be thwarted, Mehmet marshalled his boats at a cove (where Dolmabahçe Palace now stands) and had them transported overland by night on rollers, up the valley (present site of the Hilton Hotel) and down the other side into the Golden Horn at Kasımpaşa. Catching the Byzantine defenders by surprise, he soon had the Golden Horn under control.

The last great obstacle was provided by the city's mighty walls. No matter how heavily Mehmet's cannons battered them, the Byzantines rebuilt the walls by night and, come daybreak, the impetuous young sultan would find himself back where he'd started. Finally, he received a proposal from a Hungarian cannon founder called Urban who had come to help the Byzantine emperor defend Christendom against the infidels. Finding that the Byzantine emperor had no money, Urban was quick to discard his religious convictions and instead offered to make Mehmet the most enormous cannon ever seen. Mehmet gladly accepted and the mighty cannon breached the western walls, allowing the Ottomans into the city. On 28 May 1453 the final attack began, and by the evening of the 29th the Turks were in complete control of the city. The last Byzantine emperor, Constantine XI Palaiologos, died fighting on the walls.

Seeing himself as the successor to great emperors such as Constantine and Justinian, the 21-year-old conqueror at once began to rebuild and repopulate the city. Aya Sofya was converted to a mosque; a new mosque, the Fatih (Conqueror) Camii, was built on the fourth hill; and the Eski Saray (Old Palace) was constructed on the third hill, followed by a new palace (Topkapı) on Sarayburnu a few years later. The city walls were repaired and a new fortress, Yedikule, was built. İstanbul, as it began to be known, became the new administrative, commercial and cultural centre of the ever-growing Ottoman Empire.

Under Mehmet's rule, Greeks who had fled the city were encouraged to return and an imperial decree calling for resettlement was issued; Muslims, Jews and Christians all took up his offer and were promised the right to worship as they pleased. The Genoese, who had fought with the Byzantines, were pardoned and allowed to stay in Galata, though the fortifications that surrounded their settlement were torn down. Only Galata Tower was allowed to stand.

Mehmet died in 1481 and was succeeded by Beyazıt II (r 1481–1512), who was ousted by his son, the ruthless Selim the Grim (r 1512–20), famed for executing seven grand viziers and numerous relatives during his relatively short reign.

The building boom that Mehmet kicked off was continued by his successors, with Süleyman the Magnificent (r 1520–66) and his architect Mimar Sinan being responsible for an enormous amount of construction. The city was endowed with buildings

İSTANBUL IN...

Two Days

With only two days, you'll need to get cracking! On day one, visit the **Blue Mosque** (p70), **Aya Sofya** (p64) and the **Basilica Cistern** (p83) in the morning, grab lunch in Hocapaşa Sokak in Sirkeci and then spend the afternoon at **Topkapı Palace** (p72). Head to Beyoğlu in the evening.

Day two should be devoted to the Bosphorus. Board the **Long Bosphorus Tour** (p116) for a one-way trip up the Bosphorus and then make your way back to town by bus, visiting museums and monuments along the way. Afterwards, walk up through Galata to **İstiklal Caddesi** (p102) and have a drink at a rooftop bar before dinner nearby.

Four Days

Spend your third morning exploring the Bazaar District. Visit the **Süleymaniye Mosque** (p96) then follow our **Ottoman Heartland city walk** (p105) before taking a meander through the **Grand Bazaar** (p96). After lunch, head up the Golden Horn for the frescoes and mosaics of the **Kariye Mosque** (p104).

On day four brush up on history inside the **Museum of Turkish & Islamic Arts** (p90) and **İstanbul Archaeology Museum** (p91) then hop on the ferry to Kadıköy to explore the vibrant **market** (p110) and thriving cafe and **street-art** (p110) scene.

commissioned by the sultan and his family, court and grand viziers; these include the city's largest and grandest mosque, the Süleymaniye (1550). Later sultans built mosques and a series of palaces along the Bosphorus, among them Dolmabahçe.

However, what had been the most civilised city on earth in the time of Süleyman eventually declined along with the Ottoman Empire, and by the 19th century İstanbul had lost much of its former glory.

The city's decline reflected that of the sultanate. The concept of democracy, imported from the West, took off in the 19th century and the sultans were forced to make concessions towards it. In 1878 a group of educated Turks established the Committee for Union and Progress (CUP), better known as the Young Turks, to fight for the reformation of the Ottoman sultanate and the introduction of democratic reform. In 1908 they forced the sultan to abdicate and assumed governance of the empire.

In WWI the Young Turks allied themselves with the Central Powers which led to their political demise and after the war the city was occupied by British, French and Italian troops placed there in accordance with the Armistice of Mudros, which ended Ottoman participation in the war. The city was returned to Ottoman rule under the 1923 Treaty of Lausanne, which defined the borders of the modern Turkish state.

The post-WWI campaign by Mustafa Kemal (Atatürk) for independence and the reinstatement of Turkish territory in the Balkans was directed from Ankara. After the Republic was founded in 1923, the new government was set up in that city. Robbed of its status as the capital of a vast empire, İstanbul lost much of its wealth and atmosphere. The city's streets and neighbourhoods decayed, its infrastructure was neither maintained nor improved, and little economic development occurred there for the next half-century.

The Recent Past

The weak economic position of İstanbul was reflected in the rest of the country, and this led to growing dissatisfaction with a succession of governments. There were military coups in 1960 and 1971, and the late 1960s and 1970s were characterised by left-wing activism and political violence. This reached a shocking crescendo on 1 May (May Day) 1977, when there was a flare-up between rival political factions at a huge demonstration in Taksim Meydanı (Taksim Sq). Security forces intervened and approximately 40 protesters were killed.

The municipal elections of 1994 were a shock to the political establishment, with the upstart religious-right Refah Partisi (Welfare Party) winning elections across the country. Necmettin Erbakan became prime minister and Recep Tayyip Erdoğan (b 1954) became mayor of İstanbul and vowed to modernise infrastructure and restore the city to its former glory.

In 1997 Turkey's powerful National Security Council announced that Refah had flouted the constitutional ban on religion in politics and warned that the Turkish government should resign or face a military coup. Bowing to the inevitable, Prime Minister Erbakan did as the council wished. In İstanbul, Mayor Erdoğan was ousted by the secularist forces in the national government in late 1998.

National elections in April 1999 brought in a coalition government led by Bülent Ecevit's left-wing Democratic Left Party. Unfortunately for the new government, there was a spectacular collapse of the Turkish economy in 2001, leading to its electoral defeat in 2002. The victorious party was the moderate Adalet ve Kalkınma Partisi (Justice and Development Party; AKP), led by phoenix-like Recep Tayyip Erdoğan.

Elections in 2007 and 2011 had the same result, as did the municipal election in 2014. The result of the 2014 election was a disappointment to many secular and left-leaning İstanbullus, as well as to former AKP supporters who had changed their political allegiance as a result of the government's handling of the 2013 Gezi Park protests. These protests, which were staged in and around Taksim Meydanı, were initially a public response to a plan to redevelop the park, on the northeastern edge of the square, but transformed into a much larger protest by İstanbullus against what they saw as an increasingly autocratic and undemocratic Turkish government. Called in to disperse the crowd, police used tear gas and water cannons, which led to violent clashes, 8000 injuries, at least four deaths and thousands of arrests.

After Gezi, local authorities cracked down on any political demonstrations that were seen as antigovernment and made any large assemblies in or around Taksim Meydanı illegal. Local media outlets seen to be antigovernment were also targeted, with some being forceably closed or taken over by the government. Many İstanbul-based writers, journalists and editors were charged with serious crimes, including membership of a terror organisation, espionage and revealing confidential documents.

A coup d'état staged by a small faction of the military in July 2016 was defeated when members of the public took to the streets to defend the democratically elected AKP government. The government and many Turks believed that the coup had been orchestrated by US-based Islamic cleric Fethullah Gülen, a former close ally of Erdoğan. Official reprisals against anyone suspected of being a Gülenist, coup perpetrator or coup supporter were draconian, with thousands arrested, media outlets closed down and universities and schools purged.

Unsurprisingly, tourist arrivals plunged as a result of these events and the local economy collapsed. This and the ongoing government assaults on civil rights led to many Turks revising their wholehearted support for the AKP and President Erdoğan. In the 2019 Turkish local elections the AKP's grasp on power was considerably weakened, with the party losing both İstanbul and Ankara.

However, the city's newly elected mayor Ekrem İmamoğlu didn't have an easy entry to office, with the validity of his initial electoral victory in March 2019 being questioned by the AKP. A reelection in June of that year saw his winning margin increase – a major setback for President Erdoğan, who was widely believed to have pushed for the reelection in a bid to retain the AKP's power in the city.

◉ Sights

İstanbul's monuments have been wowing visitors ever since Roman times, and its portfolio of historic buildings, museums, markets and art galleries is nothing less than extraordinary. Indeed, there are so many top-drawer sights that there is little chance of any visitor seeing them on one visit. The only solution is to identify those that are of paramount interest and use these as lynchpins when planning your explorations through the major neighbourhoods.

◉ Sultanahmet

Constantinople (İstanbul) has been the capital of three major empires. The legacy of this can be seen everywhere you look in Sultanahmet, from decaying remnants of ancient monuments to magnificently restored grand mosques and palaces that soar skywards. In a few days you can cover the highlights of a city that took the Romans, Byzantines and Ottomans more than 1500 years to build.

★**Aya Sofya**   MUSEUM
See p64.

THE GREAT PALACE OF BYZANTIUM

Constantine the Great built the Great Palace soon after he declared Constantinople to be the capital of the Roman Empire in AD 330. Successive Byzantine leaders left their mark by adding to it, and the complex eventually consisted of hundreds of buildings over six levels. These included throne rooms, audience chambers, churches, chapels, stadiums and thermal baths, all enclosed by walls and set in terraced parklands stretching from the Hippodrome over to Hagia Sophia (Aya Sofya) and down the slope, ending at the sea walls on the Sea of Marmara. The palace was finally abandoned after the Fourth Crusade sacked the city in 1204, and its ruins were pillaged and filled in after the Conquest, becoming the foundations of much of what is known as Sultanahmet and Cankurtaran today.

Various pieces of the Great Palace have been uncovered – many by budding hotelier 'archaeologists'. The mosaics in the **Museum of Great Palace Mosaics** (Büyük Saray Mozaikleri Müzesi; Map p88; ✆0212-518 1205; www.ayasofyamuzesi.gov.tr/en/museum-great-palace-mosaics; Torun Sokak; adult/child under 8yr ₺24/free; ☺9am-6.30pm Apr-Sep, to 4.30pm Oct-Mar; ⛴Sultanahmet) once graced the floor of the complex, and excavations at the sadly dilapidated **Sultanahmet Archaeological Park** (Map p88; Kabasakal Caddesi; ⛴Sultanahmet) near Aya Sofya have uncovered other parts of the palace.

For more information, check out www.byzantium1200.com, which has computer-generated images that bring ancient Byzantium to life.

★ **Basilica Cistern**   HISTORIC SITE
(Yerebatan Sarnıçı; Map p88; ✆0212-512 1570; www.yerebatan.com; Yerebatan Caddesi; adult/child under 8yr ₺20/free; ☺9am-5.30pm Nov-mid-Apr, to 6.30pm mid-Apr–Oct; ⛴Sultanahmet) This subterranean structure was commissioned by Emperor Justinian and built in 532. The largest surviving Byzantine cistern in İstanbul, Basilica Cistern was constructed using 336 columns, many of which were salvaged from ruined temples and feature fine carved capitals. Its symmetry and sheer grandeur of conception are quite breathtaking, and its cavernous depths make it a great retreat on scorching summer days.

Like most sites in İstanbul, the cistern has an unusual history. It was originally known as the Basilica Cistern because it lay underneath the Stoa Basilica, one of the great squares on the first hill. Designed to service the Great Palace and surrounding buildings, it was able to store up to 80,000 cu metres of water delivered via 20km of aqueducts from a reservoir near the Black Sea, but was closed when the Byzantine emperors relocated from the Great Palace. Forgotten by the city authorities some time before the Conquest, it wasn't rediscovered until 1545, when scholar Petrus Gyllius was researching Byzantine antiquities in the city and was told by local residents that they were able to obtain water by lowering buckets into a dark space below their basement floors. Some were even catching fish this way. Intrigued, Gyllius explored the neighbourhood and finally accessed the cistern through one of the basements. Even after his discovery, the Ottomans (who referred to the cistern as Yerebatan Saray) didn't treat the so-called Underground Palace with the respect it deserved – it became a dumping ground for all sorts of junk, as well as corpses.

The cistern was cleaned and renovated in 1985 by the İstanbul Metropolitan Municipality and opened to the public in 1987. It's now one of the city's most popular tourist attractions. Walking along its raised wooden platforms, you'll feel water dripping from the vaulted ceiling and see schools of ghostly carp patrolling the water – it certainly has bucketloads of atmosphere. Note that the Museum Pass İstanbul isn't accepted here.

Hippodrome   PARK
(Atmeydanı; Map p88; Atmeydanı Caddesi; ⛴Sultanahmet) The Byzantine emperors loved nothing more than an afternoon at the chariot races, and this rectangular arena alongside Sultanahmet Park was their venue of choice. In its heyday, it was decorated by obelisks and statues, some of which remain in place today. Re-landscaped in more recent years, it is one of the city's most popular meeting places and promenades. Originally the arena consisted of two levels of

İstanbul

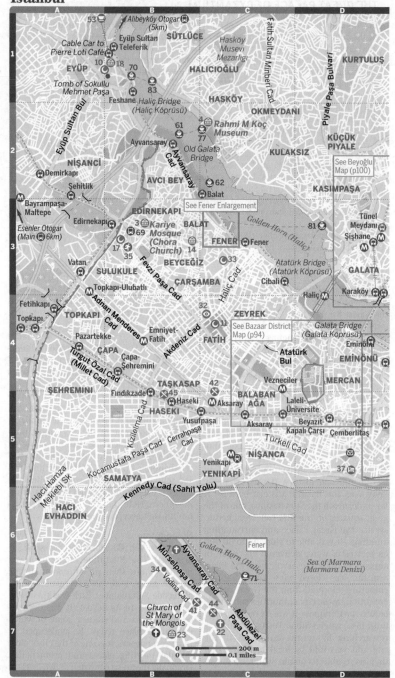

İSTANBUL

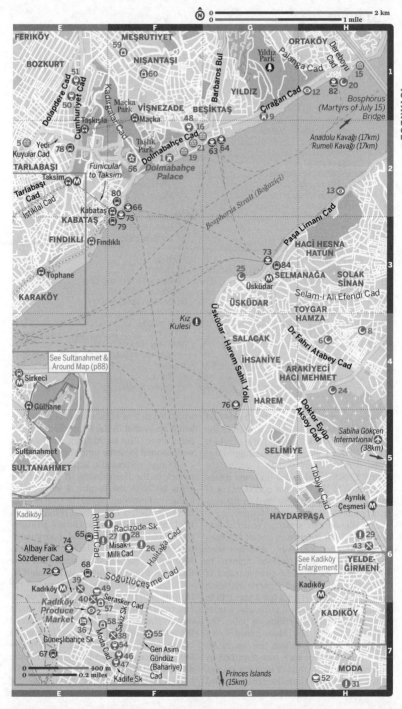

FERİKÖY

BOZKURT

MEŞRUTİYET

59

NIŞANTAŞI
60

YILDIZ
Yıldız
Park

ORTAKÖY
Palanga Cad
Dereboyu Cad
15
20
82

Bosphorus
(Martyrs of July 15)
Bridge

Çırağan Cad
12
9

Anadolu Kavağı (17km)
Rumeli Kavağı (17km)

51
50
Dolapdere Cad
Cumhuriyet Cad
Taşkışla

5
Yedi
Kuyular Cad
78

Maçka
Park
VİŞNEZADE
Maçka
48

Barbaros Bul
BEŞİKTAŞ
16

Kadırgalar Cad
Taşlık
Park
Dolmabahçe Cad
1
19
21
56
63 64

TARLABAŞI

Funicular
to Taksim
Dolmabahçe
Palace

13

Tarlabaşı
Cad
Taksim
İstiklal Cad

80

KABATAŞ
66
Kabataş
75
79

Bosphorus Strait (Boğaziçi)

Paşa Limanı Cad

FINDIKLI
Fındıklı

73
84

HACİ HESNA
HATUN

25
SELMANAĞA
Üsküdar

SOLAK
SİNAN

Tophane

KARAKÖY

ÜSKÜDAR

Selam-i Ali Efendi Cad

TOYGAR
HAMZA

Kız
Kulesi

Üsküdar - Harem Sahil Yolu

SALACAK

İHSANİYE

Dr Fahri Atabey Cad
6
8

See Sultanahmet &
Around Map (p88)

Sirkeci

Gülhane

ARAKIYECİ
HACI MEHMET
24

76

HAREM

Doktor Eyüp
Aksoy Cad

Sabiha Gökçen
International
(38km)

Sultanahmet

SULTANAHMET

SELİMİYE

Tıbbiye Cad

Ayrılık
Çeşmesi

HAYDARPAŞA

29
43

See Kadıköy
Enlargement

YELDE-
ĞİRMENİ

Kadıköy

KADIKÖY

Kadıköy

30

Racizode Sk

Rıhtım Cad

74
65

27
28

Albay Faik
Sözdener Cad

Misak-ı
Milli Cad
26

Halitağa Cad

72

68

Söğütlüçeşme Cad

39

Kadıköy

49

40

Serasker Cad

Kadıköy
Produce
Market

2

57

36

54
58

Sakız Sk

Moda Cad

38

55

Gen Asim
Gündüz
(Bahariye)
Cad

Güneşlibahçe Sk

67

46
47

Kadife Sk

0   400 m
0   0.2 miles

Princes Islands
(15km)

MODA

52

31

0   2 km
0   1 mile

İstanbul

galleries, a central spine, starting boxes and the semicircular southern end known as the **Sphendone** (Nakilbent Sokak), parts of which still stand. The galleries that once topped this stone structure were damaged during the Fourth Crusade and ended up being totally dismantled in the Ottoman period; many of the original columns were used in the construction of the Süleymaniye Mosque.

The Hippodrome was the centre of Byzantium's life for 1000 years and of Ottoman life for another 400 years, and has been the scene of countless political dramas. In Byzantine times, the rival chariot teams of 'Greens' and 'Blues' had separate sectarian connections. Support for a team was akin to membership of a political party, and a team victory had important effects on policy. Occasionally, Greens and Blues joined forces against the emperor, as was the case in AD 532 when a chariot race was disturbed by protests against Justinian's high tax regime. This escalated into the Nika riots (so called after the protesters' cry of *Nika!*, or Victory!),

which led to tens of thousands of protesters being massacred in the Hippodrome by imperial forces. Not surprisingly, chariot races were banned for some time afterwards.

Ottoman sultans also kept an eye on activities in the Hippodrome. If things were going badly in the empire, a surly crowd gathering here could signal the start of a disturbance, then a riot, then a revolution. In 1826 the slaughter of the corrupt janissary corps (the sultan's personal bodyguards) was carried out here by the reformer Sultan Mahmut II. In 1909 there were riots here that caused the downfall of Abdül Hamit II.

Despite the ever-present threat of the Hippodrome being the scene of their downfall, emperors and sultans sought to outdo one another in beautifying it, and adorned the centre with statues from the far reaches of the empire. Unfortunately, many priceless statues carved by ancient masters have disappeared from their original homes here. Chief among those responsible for such thefts were the soldiers of the Fourth

Crusade, who invaded Constantinople, a Christian ally city, in 1204.

Near the northern end of the Hippodrome, the little gazebo with beautiful stonework is known as **Kaiser Wilhelm's Fountain**. The German emperor paid a state visit to Sultan Abdül Hamit II in 1898, and presented this fountain to the sultan and his people as a token of friendship in 1901. The monograms on the dome's interior feature Abdül Hamit's *tuğra* (calligraphic signature) and the first letter of Wilhelm's name, representing their political union.

The immaculately preserved pink granite **Obelisk of Theodosius** in the centre was carved in Egypt during the reign of Thutmose III (r 1549–1503 BC) and erected in the Amon-Re temple at Karnak. Theodosius the Great (r 379–95) had it brought from Egypt to Constantinople in AD 390. On the marble podium below the obelisk, look for the carvings of Theodosius, his wife, his sons, state officials and bodyguards watching the chariot-race action from the *kathisma* (imperial box).

South of the obelisk is a strange column coming up out of a hole in the ground. Known as the **Spiral Column**, it was once much taller and was topped by three serpents' heads. Originally cast to commemorate a victory of the Hellenic confederation over the Persians in the battle of Plataea, it stood in front of the Temple of Apollo at Delphi (Greece) from 478 BC until Constantine the Great had it brought to his new capital city around AD 330. Though badly damaged in Byzantine times, the serpents' heads survived until the early 18th century. Now all that remains of them is one upper jaw, which was discovered in a basement of Aya Sofya and is housed in the İstanbul Archaeology Museums (p91).

After sacking Aya Sofya in 1204, the soldiers of the Fourth Crusade tore all the plates from the **Rough-Stone Obelisk**, at the Hippodrome's southern end, in the mistaken belief that they were solid gold (in fact, they were gold-covered bronze). The Crusaders also stole the famous

Sultanahmet & Around

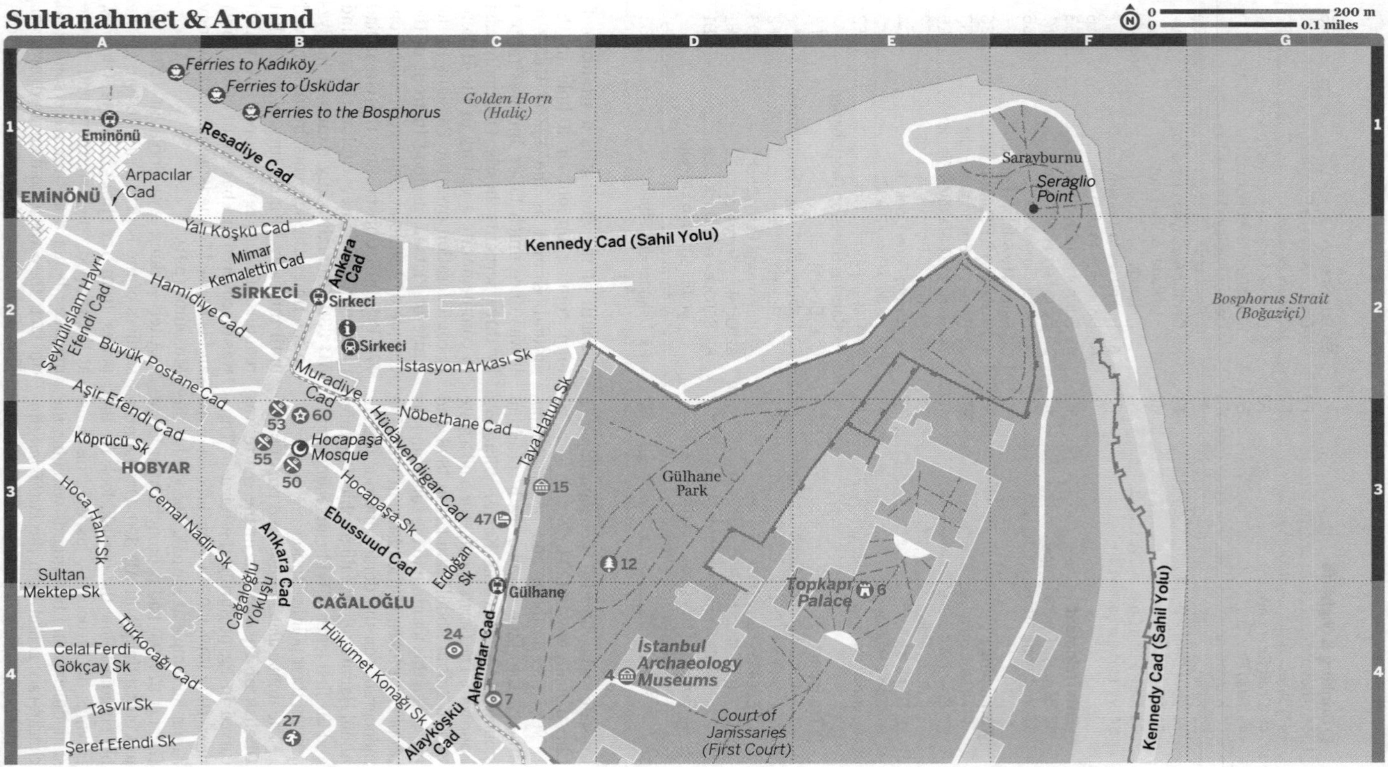

N 0 — 200 m
0 — 0.1 miles

Bosphorus Strait (Boğaziçi)

Golden Horn (Haliç)

Ferries to Kadıköy
Ferries to Üsküdar
Ferries to the Bosphorus

EMİNÖNÜ

Eminönü

Sarayburnu

Seraglio Point

Kennedy Cad (Sahil Yolu)

Kennedy Cad (Sahil Yolu)

Reşadiye Cad

Arpacılar Cad

Yalı Köşkü Cad
Mimar Kemalettin Cad
Hamidiye Cad

Seyhülislam Hayri Efendi Cad

Büyük Postane Cad

Aşir Efendi Cad

Köprücü Sk

HOBYAR

Hoca Hanı Sk

Cemal Nadir Sk

Sultan Mektep Sk

Celal Ferdi Gökçay Sk

Türkocağı Cad

Tasvir Sk

Şeref Efendi Sk

Ankara Cad

Çataloğlu Yokuşu

Ankara Cad

Hükümet Konağı Sk

CAĞALOĞLU

27

Alayköşkü Cad

7

Hüdavendigar Cad

Nobethane Cad

İstasyon Arkası Sk

Muradiye Cad

Sirkeci

SİRKECİ

Sirkeci

53 60
55 50

Hocapaşa Mosque

Hocapaşa Sk

Ebussuud Cad

24

47

Erdoşin Sk

Taya Hatun Sk

15

Gülhane

Gülhane Park

12

İstanbul Archaeology Museums

Court of Janissaries (First Court)

Topkapı Palace

6

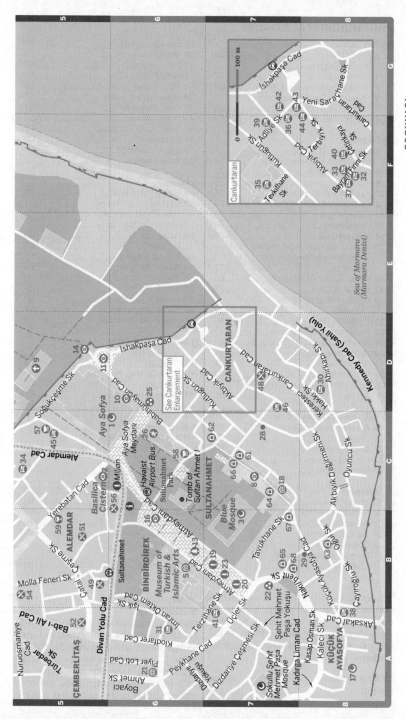

Cankurtaran Enlargement

0 — 100 m

İshakpaşa Cad
Yeni Saraçhane Sk
Cankurtaran Cad
Adliye Sk
Çetinkaya Sk
Kutlugün Sk
Akbıyık Cad
Terbıyık Sk
Tevkifhane Sk
Bayram Fırını Cad

Sea of Marmara
(Marmara Denizi)

Kennedy Cad (Sahil Yolu)

İshakpaşa Cad

CANKURTARAN

See Cankurtaran
Enlargement

Kutlugün Sk
Akbıyık Cad
Cankurtaran Cad

Kırkçeşme Cad
Hakkı Sk
Ahırkapı Sk

Oyuncu Sk

Akbıyık Değirmeni Sk

Söğükçeşme Sk
Alemdar Cad
Yerebatan Cad
Basilica
Cistern
ALEMDAR

Molla Feneri Sk
Celal Çeşme Sk
Sultanahmet

Nuruosmaniye Cad
Türbedar Sk
Bab-ı Ali Cad
ÇEMBERLİTAŞ

Divan Yolu Cad
Klodfarer Cad
Piyer Loti Cad
Boyacı Ahmet Sk
BİNBİRDİREK

Museum of
Turkish &
Islamic Arts

Aya Sofya
Aya Sofya
Meydanı
Milion
Havaist
Airport Bus
Sultanahmet
Park
Babıhümayun Cad

Tomb of
Sultan Ahmet I

SULTANAHMET

Blue
Mosque

İmran Öktem Cad
Atmeydanı Cad
Terzihane Sk
Üçler Sk
Dizdariye Çeşmesi Sk
Peykhane Cad

Sokullu Şehit
Mehmet Paşa Mosque
Dizdariye Yokuşu
Şehit Mehmet
Paşa Yokuşu
Tavukhane Sk
Nakilbent Sk

Kadırga Limanı Cad
Kasap Osman Sk
Kaleci Sk
Küçük Ayasofya Cad
KÜÇÜK
AYASOFYA
Aksakal Cad
Çayıroğlu Sk
Küçük Ayasofya Cad
Oğul Sk

Sultanahmet & Around

Triumphal Quadriga (team of four horses cast in bronze) and placed it atop the main door of Venice's Basilica di San Marco; replicas are now located there, as the originals were moved into the basilica for safekeeping.

★ **Blue Mosque**   MOSQUE
See p70.

★ **Museum of Turkish
& Islamic Arts**   MUSEUM
(Türk ve Islam Eserleri Müzesi; Map p88; ☑ 0212-518 1805; www.muze.gov.tr; Atmeydanı Caddesi 46, Hippodrome; adult/child under 8yr ₺42/free; ◔ 9am-6.30pm Apr-Sep, to 4pm Tue-Sun Oct-Mar; ◻ Sultanahmet) This Ottoman palace was built in 1524 for İbrahim Paşa, childhood friend, brother-in-law and grand vizier of

Süleyman the Magnificent. It now houses a splendid collection of artefacts, including exquisite calligraphy and one of the world's most impressive antique carpet collections. The collection is a knockout with its palace carpets, prayer rugs and glittering artefacts, such as a 17th-century Ottoman incense burner.

Born in Greece, İbrahim Paşa was captured in that country as a child and sold as a slave into the imperial household in İstanbul. He worked as a page in Topkapı Palace, where he became friendly with Süleyman, who was the same age. When his friend became sultan, İbrahim was made in turn chief falconer, chief of the royal bedchamber and grand vizier. This palace was bestowed on him by Süleyman the year before he was given the hand of Süleyman's sister, Hadice, in marriage. Alas, the fairy tale was not to last for poor İbrahim. His wealth, power and influence on the monarch became so great that others wishing to influence the sultan became envious, chief among them Süleyman's powerful wife, Haseki Hürrem Sultan (Roxelana). After a rival accused İbrahim of disloyalty, Roxelana convinced her husband that İbrahim was a threat and Süleyman had him strangled in 1536.

Artefacts in the museum's collection date from the 8th to the 19th century and come from across the Middle East. They include *müknames* (scrolls outlining an imperial decree) featuring the sultan's *tuğra* (calligraphic signature); Iranian book binding from the Safavid period (1501–1722); 12th- and 13th-century wooden columns and doors from Damascus and Cizre; Holbein, Lotto, Konya, Uşhak, Iran and Caucasia carpets; and even a cutting of the Prophet's beard. Sections of the Hippodrome walls can be seen near the entrance.

Arasta Bazaar MARKET

(Map p88; off Torun Sokak; ⓐSultanahmet) This historic arcade of shops was once part of the *külliye* (mosque complex) of the Blue Mosque (Sultanahmet Camii). Mosques built by the great and powerful usually included numerous public-service institutions, including an *arasta* (row of shops) such as this, as well as hospitals, soup kitchens and schools. The *arasta* is now home to some of Sultanahmet's most alluring boutiques.

Little Aya Sofya MOSQUE

(Küçük Aya Sofya Camii, SS Sergius & Bacchus Church; Map p88; Küçük Ayasofya Caddesi, Küçük Ayasofya; ☉sunrise-sunset; ⓐSultanahmet, Çemberlitaş) **FREE** Justinian and his wife Theodora built this little church sometime between 527 and 536, just before Justinian built Aya Sofya. You can still see their monogram worked into some of the frilly white capitals. The building is one of the most beautiful Byzantine structures in the city despite being converted into a mosque in the early 16th century and having many of its original features obscured during an extensive restoration in 2007.

★Topkapı Palace PALACE

See p72.

★İstanbul Archaeology Museums MUSEUM

(İstanbul Arkeoloji Müzeleri; Map p88; ☏0212-520 7740; www.muze.gov.tr; Osman Hamdi Bey Yokuşu Sokak, Gülhane; adult/child under 8yr ₺36/free; ☉9am-7pm Tue-Sun Apr-Sep, to 4.30pm Tue-Sun Oct-Mar; ⓐGülhane) The city's foremost archaeological museum is housed in three buildings close to Topkapı Palace. There are many highlights, but the sarcophagi from the Royal Necropolis of Sidon are particularly striking. Currently undergoing a massive renovation, much of the main building is closed and only the Tiled Pavilion, Museum of the Ancient Orient and Ancient Age Sculpture section (where the sarcophagi are displayed) can be visited.

The complex has three main parts: the Museum of the Ancient Orient (Eski Şark Eserler Müzesi), the Archaeology Museum (Arkeoloji Müzesi) and the Tiled Pavilion (Çinili Köşk). These museums house the palace collections formed during the late 19th century by museum director, artist and archaeologist Osman Hamdi Bey. The complex can be easily reached by walking down the slope from Topkapı's First Court, or by walking up the hill from the main gate of Gülhane Park.

➡ **Museum of the Ancient Orient**
Located immediately on the left after you enter the complex, this 1883 building has a collection of pre-Islamic items gathered from the expanse of the Ottoman Empire. Highlights include an 8th-century BC Hittite moulding of a rock relief depicting the storm god Tarhunza and a series of large

İSTANBUL SIGHTS

İSTANBUL'S CONTEMPORARY ART SCENE

İstanbul Modern (İstanbul Modern Sanat Müzesi; Map p100; ☑0212-334 7300; www.istanbul modern.org; Meşrutiyet Caddesi 99, Asmalımescit; adult/student/child under 12yr ₺72/54/free; ⊙10am-6pm Tue, Wed, Fri & Sat, to 8pm Thu, 11am-8pm Sun; Ⓜ Şişhane, ⓐ Tünel) This lavishly funded and innovative museum has an extensive collection of Turkish art and also stages a constantly changing and uniformly excellent program of mixed-media exhibitions by high-profile local and international artists. Its permanent home is next to the Bosphorus in Tophane, but the massive Galataport redevelopment project currently under way has led to it temporarily relocating to this site in Beyoğlu.

ARTER (Map p84; ☑0212-708 5800; www.arter.org.tr; Irmak Caddesi 13, Dolapdere; adult/ child & student ₺25/15, free on Thu; ⊙11am-7pm Tue-Sun, to 8pm Thu, extended hours 1st Sat of month; ⓐ54KT from Taksim) Opened to great fanfare in September 2019, the new home of the Koç Foundation's collection of contemporary art – one of the most impressive in Turkey – was designed by London-based Grimshaw Architects and is located 1km north-west of Taksim Sq, in the Dolapdere district. It incorporates exhibition spaces, a sculp-ture terrace, performance halls, a library, an arts bookstore and a cafe, and its exhibition program is sure to be as impressive as its six-floor building, which has a shimmering facade of glass-fibre mosaics. Free shuttle buses run from the Taksim metro station and Pera Museum in Tepebaşı; check the website for details.

SALT Beyoğlu (Map p100; ☑0212-377 4200; www.saltonline.org; İstiklal Caddesi 136; ⊙noon-8pm Tue-Sat, to 6pm Sun; Ⓜ Şişhane, ⓐ Tünel) With a brief to explore critical and timely issues in visual and material culture, the İstiklal branch of the SALT cultural centre is one of the city's most interesting arts-focused institutions. Occupying a former apart-ment building dating from the 1850s, it houses exhibition spaces, a cinema, a bookshop and a reading room popular with students. Exhibitions tend to be dominated by photo-graphic and multimedia works.

Galata Rum Okulu (Galata Greek School; Map p100; www.galatarumokulu.blogspot.com.tr; Kemeraltı Caddesi 25, Tophane; ⊙noon-6pm Tue-Sat; ⓐ Tophane) With works displayed under glass on top of worn wooden desks or lecterns, and exhibition titles written on black-boards, the historical atmosphere of the former Greek Primary School – now a venue for shows by local contemporary artists – often becomes part of the visual experience. The space also hosts big art events, occasional conferences and lectures.

Anna Laudel Contemporary (Map p100; ☑0212-243 3257; www.annalaudel.gallery; Bankalar Caddesi 10, Karaköy; ⊙noon-7pm Tue-Sat, to 6pm Sun; ⓐ Karaköy) Contemporary Turkish and international artists are featured in the shows at this gallery space, opened in late 2016 in one of the historic buildings in İstanbul's old finance district. Though the gallery covers five floors, each is small, making for an intimate viewing experience. A shop sells jewellery, prints and other small artworks.

Depo (Map p100; ☑0212-292 3956; www.depoistanbul.net; Lüleci Hendek Caddesi 12, To-phane; ⊙11am-7pm Tue-Sun; ⓐ Tophane) Occupying a former tobacco warehouse, this alternative space is operated by Anadolu Kültür (www.anadolukultur.org), a not-for-profit organisation that facilitates artistic collaboration, promotes cultural exchange and stimulates debates on social and political issues relevant to Turkey, the South Caucasus, the Middle East and the Balkans. It hosts a wide range of talks, art exhibi-tions and film screenings.

blue-and-yellow glazed-brick panels that once lined the processional street and the Ishtar gate of ancient Babylon. The latter de-pict real and mythical animals such as lions, dragons and bulls.

➡ **Archaeology Museum**

On the opposite side of the column-filled courtyard to the Museum of the Ancient Orient is this imposing neoclassical build-ing, parts of which were undergoing renova-tion when we visited. It houses an extensive collection of classical statuary and sarcophagi plus exhibits documenting İstanbul's ancient, Byzantine and Ottoman history.

The museum's major treasures are sarcophagi from sites including the Royal Necropolis of Sidon (Side in modern-day Lebanon), unearthed in 1887 by Osman Hamdi Bey. Don't miss the extraordinary *Alexander Sarcophagus* and *Mourning Women Sarcophagus*. The northern wing of the museum houses an impressive collection of ancient grave-cult sarcophagi from Syria, Lebanon, Thessalonica and Ephesus (Efes), including impressive **anthropoid sarcophagi** from Sidon. Three halls are filled with the amazingly detailed stelae and sarcophagi, most dating from between AD 140 and 270. Many of the sarcophagi look like tiny temples or residential buildings; don't miss the **Sidamara Sarcophagus** from Konya (3rd century AD) with its interlocking horses' legs and playful cherubs. The last room in this section contains Roman floor mosaics and examples of Anatolian architecture from antiquity.

➡ **Tiled Pavilion**

The last of the complex's museum buildings is this handsome pavilion, constructed in 1472 by order of Mehmet the Conqueror. The portico, which has 14 marble columns, was constructed during the reign of Sultan Abdül Hamit I (1774–89) after the original burned down in 1737.

On display here are Seljuk, Anatolian and Ottoman tiles and ceramics dating from the end of the 12th century to the beginning of the 20th century. The collection includes İznik tiles from the period between the mid-14th and 17th centuries when that city produced the finest coloured tiles in the world. When you enter the central room you can't miss the stunning *mihrab* from the İbrahim Bey İmâret in Karaman, built in 1432.

Gülhane Park   PARK
(Gülhane Parkı; Map p88; ⊙7am-10pm; 🚇Gülhane) Gülhane Park was once part of the grounds of Topkapı Palace, accessible only to the royal court. These days crowds of locals come here to picnic under the many trees, promenade past the formally planted flowerbeds, and enjoy wonderful views of the Bosphorus, Sea of Marmara and Princes' Islands from the park's northeastern edge. The park is especially lovely during the İstanbul Tulip Festival (p119), when thousands of tulips bloom.

Next to the southern entrance is the Alay Köşkü (Parade Kiosk), now open to the public as the **Ahmet Hamdi Tanpınar Literature Museum Library** (Ahmet Hamdi Tanpınar Edebiyat Müze Kütüphanesi; Map p88; ☑0212-520 2081; http://ahtem.kutuphane.gov.tr; ⊙8.30am-8.30pm Mon-Sat) **FREE**. Inside, next to the western walls is the **İstanbul Museum of the History of Science & Technology in Islam** (İstanbul İslam Bilim ve Teknoloji Tarihi Müzesi; Map p88; ☑0212-528 8065; www.ibttm.org; Has Ahırlar Binaları; adult/child under 8yr ₺14/free; ⊙9am-7pm Apr-Sep, to 4.15pm Oct-Mar).

Across the street from the main park entrance and 100m downhill from the park's main gate is an outrageously curvaceous rococo gate leading into the precincts of what was once the grand vizierate, or Ottoman prime ministry, known in the West as the **Sublime Porte** (Map p88; Alemdar Caddesi) thanks to this flamboyant entrance. Today the buildings beyond the gate hold various offices of the İstanbul provincial government (the Vilayetler).

◎ Bazaar District

Crowned by the city's first and most evocative shopping mall – the famous Grand Bazaar (Kapalı Çarşı) – the Bazaar District is also home to three of the grandest of all Ottoman buildings, the Süleymaniye, Yenı (New) and Beyazıt Mosques.

Aqueduct of Valens   LANDMARK
(Map p94; Atatürk Bulvarı, Zeyrek; Ⓜ Vezneciler) Rising majestically over the traffic on busy Atatürk Bulvarı, this limestone aqueduct is one of the city's most distinctive landmarks. Commissioned by Emperor Valens and completed in AD 378, it linked the third and fourth hills and carried water to a cistern at Beyazıt Meydanı before finally ending up at the **Great Palace of Byzantium**.

The aqueduct was part of an elaborate system sourcing water from the north of the city and linking more than 250km of water channels, some 30 bridges and more than 100 cisterns within the city walls, making it one of the greatest hydraulic engineering achievements of ancient times. After the Conquest, it supplied the Eski (Old) and Topkapı Palaces with water.

Bazaar District

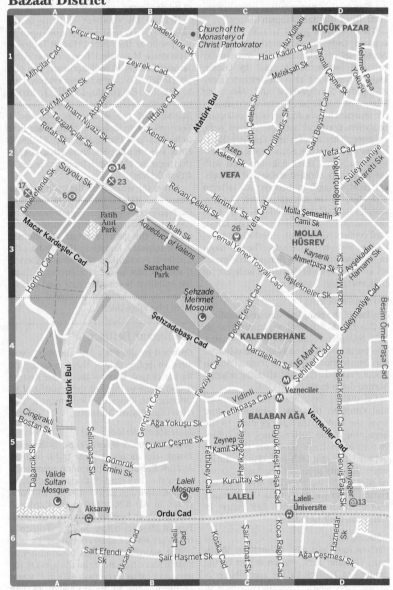

Women's Bazaar
MARKET

(Kadınlar Pazarı; Map p94; İtfaiye Caddesi, Zeyrek; Ⓜ Vezneciler) Though it's a wonderful spot to observe local life, the vibrant Women's Bazaar isn't for the faint-hearted. Freshly slaughtered sheep carcasses swing in the wind and shops sell dried sheep heads, pungent *tulum* cheese and other unusual produce. Most shopkeepers are from the southeastern corner of Turkey – specifically Siirt – and the tasty food served at the bazaar's eateries reflects this. It's open daily though hours vary between the various shops.